Contents

Foreword	v
Seismology	1
Seismoscopes	2
Seismographs and Seismometers	3
Seismograms	9
Miscellaneous	9
Atmospheric Electricity	10
Electrometers	11
Telegraph Line Protectors	13
Lightning Conductors for Buildings	14
Miscellaneous	14
Gravity	16
Pendulum Apparatus	17
Torsion Apparatus	20
Miscellaneous	21
Tide Measurement	22
Tide Gauges	23
Tidal Analysis and Prediction	24
Miscellaneous	25
Geomagnetism	26
Variation Compasses	27
Dip circles	29
Kew Pattern Unifilar Magnetometers	32
Observatory Magnetometers	32
Inertia Rings and Bars	35
Terrellae and Magnetic Models	35
Miscellaneous	36
Research in the Ionosphere	36
Geophysical Prospecting	37
Exploration Seismographs	38
Creating and detecting seismic waves	38
Exploration gravity meters	39
Exploration magnetometers	41
Electrical prospecting methods	43
Miscellaneous	44
Maker's Index	45

iii

Foreword

Geophysics is the science dealing with the physical properties of the earth in its entirety. The Museum's Geophysics Collections contain instruments and apparatus for investigating the structure of the solid earth, its gravity, magnetic and electrical fields, and its tides. We collect also similar apparatus designed for geophysical prospecting, where local variations of the same parameters reveal aspects of regional subsurface geology.

The collection has come from many sources, private, commercial and academic. However much geophysical research has always been directed at national level and the Museum has benefited from its own national status whereby apparatus from the Admiralty, the Royal Society, and the major government-funded observatories has come into our care.

The Museum has other Earth Science Collections: namely, Meteorology and Oceanography, whilst instruments similar to those in the Geophysics Collections, though usually having a different purpose, can be found in the Electricity & Magnetism, Surveying, Navigation and Astronomy Collections.

London Borough
of Enfield
Public Libraries

Z05630

Seismology

The basic problem in measuring ground motion is to find a place to stand from which to observe the movement of the earth. Since the seismologist has no place to stand except the very earth whose motion he seeks to measure, he must resort to a different procedure to make these observations. The commonest method is to set up a mass with a minimum of attachment to the earth and to depend on its inertia to keep it in position as the earth moves. The simplest type of seismometer uses a pendulum whose mass tends to stand still as the supporting frame moves. In practice, the suspended system does move, but as long as there is relative motion between the ground and its support, ground motion can be detected. The terms 'seismometer' and 'seismoscope' refer to this type of apparatus, which will register the occurrence of a shock wave but not its duration. The Chang Hêng seismoscope is an example of such a device in its simplest form.

In the middle of the 18th century two events stimulated the study of earthquakes: the series of strong shocks felt in England during the 1750s and the Lisbon earthquake of 1755 which destroyed that city. Many catalogues of past earthquakes were compiled and theories put foward to account for their cause. Some naturalists tried to correlate the occurrence of earthquakes with various seasons or phases of the moon; others listed their effects and distinguished between those due to volcanic eruptions and those having other origins.

In the late 18th and early 19th centuries systematic investigations were carried out on site following notable earthquakes and this led to theoretical calculations of earthquake wave velocity and of the origin and depth of observed shocks. From the middle of the 19th century Italian scientists were leaders in earthquake studies. They set up observatories and founded a journal. Efforts were made to devise an instrument which would record the shocks and indicate the duration and the direction from which they came.

During the early 19th century seismographs were built using simple pendulums like those fitted to long-case clocks, but these proved insensitive as relative motion between the pendulum and its support was too small to be useful. Eventually it was realised that a short horizontal pendulum could successfully replace a long vertical one, and other suspended systems also proved effective: mainly inverted, torsion, and vertical-spring systems. With a sensitive electrical detecting system the mass can be reduced to a few grams. In such cases the instrument must be shielded from all local disturbances and changes of temperature.

The first seismographs from whose readings the times, directions, and velocities of near and distant earthquake shocks could be deduced were designed in Japan during the last quarter of the 19th century by three British scientists who were teaching there: John Milne, James Ewing and Thomas Gray. The term 'seismograph' denotes an instrument which can make a continuous record of the movement of its pendulum, with reference to a time-mark, so that the exact arrival of each wave may be determined.

Such recordings may be mechanical, photographic, or electrical; the latter two methods having the advantage of being without friction.

If the seismometer is 'tuned' to certain wave lengths, it can serve civil engineers as a vibration-recorder or tiltmeter. Geophysicists use portable seismographs to record waves from controlled explosions which are reflected and refracted from the upper layers of rocks. A global network of seismographs records the waves that have travelled through and around the earth; from their records we can deduce the internal structure of the globe.

Three pendulums are generally needed to pick up the horizontal and vertical components of ground motion: the first two being aligned East-West and North-South, and the latter able to move in the vertical plane.

Seismoscopes

Chang Hêng's Seismoscope, 132 AD (Sectioned reconstruction)
Height overall: 37 cm
See also:
1976–312 Another reconstruction illustrated on a Chinese postage stamp.
1980–712 Porcelain statue of Chang Hêng.

Based on contemporary descriptions of a seismoscope devised by the Chinese geographer and astronomer Chang Hêng (78–139). Arriving shock waves displaced a heavy pendulum linked to the mechanism which opens the jaws of that dragon's head facing the direction of the earthquake. This action released a ball into the mouth of a toad seated below, serving to record the event.

Inv. no. 1976-107   Neg. nos. 734/76, 735/76
Source: British Broadcasting Corporation

Von Lasaulx Seismochronoscope 1876
Width overall: 16 cm

A mechanical device consisting of a balanced cup-and-ball linked to a rod. Set up beside a pendulum clock the ball was dislodged by earth tremors and the rod fell against the pendulum, stopping the clock and thus indicating the time of the tremor.

Inv. no. 1876-1219
Source: Purchased from Prof. Von Lasaulx

Seismoscope by Brassart, 1884
Height overall: 33 cm

Designed by Tacchini, it was installed at several observatories around Mt Etna in Sicily. A ball-and-rod left of the clock was upset by the arrival of horizontal shock waves and falling into one angle of the surrounding ring marked with compass points, indicated the general direction of the first shock. Vertical motion caused the long spring to stretch and its terminal bob to dip into a copper cup of mercury. Either action completed an electrical circuit which rang a bell and started the clock.

Inv. nos. 1884-63, 1884-64   Neg. no. 294/56
Source: Purchased from Brassart

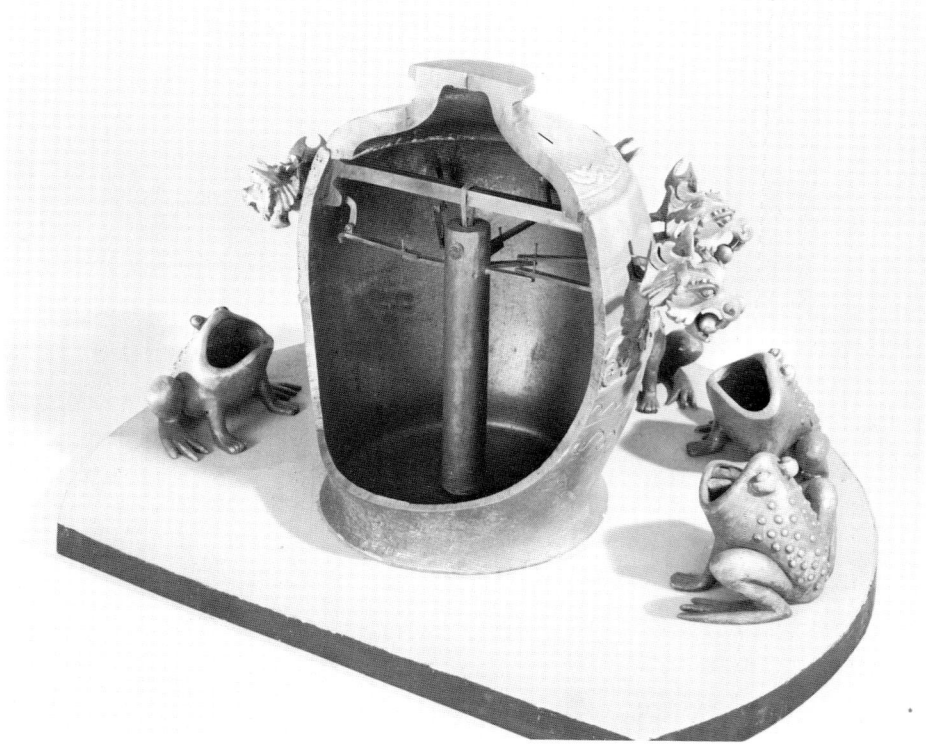

Chang Hêng's Seismoscope, 132 AD

Seismoscope by Brassart, 1884

Seismographs and Seismometers

Ewing Three-component Seismograph, 1880
Height overall: 119 cm
Plate diameter: 60 cm
See also: 1921–1055, seismogram (Tokyo 1877) page 9.

Designed by Sir Alfred Ewing and made by the Cambridge Scientific Instrument Co. This is a composite instrument: a small seismoscope fitted with an electromagnetic detent, reacts to the first shockwaves, starting the clockwork drive of the main seismograph plate. Subsequent vertical and horizontal components of ground motion are detected, magnified, and scribed on a smoked glass plate. A clock, also set running by the seismoscope, marks the plate at 1-second intervals during its first revolution.

Inv. no. 1888-173   Neg. no. 293/56
Source: Purchased from Cambridge Sci. Inst. Co

Gray-Milne Seismograph, 1885
Height overall: 77 cm

This continuously-running seismograph was designed by Thomas Gray and John Milne, and made by James White of Glasgow. Clockwork drives a paper band on which glass-siphon pens register the three components of ground motion. The time of occurrence and the oscillation period are obtained from the time-mark line which also serves as datum for measuring any shift in the pendulum bobs caused by ground tilt.

Inv. no. 1885-115
Neg. nos. 1242/54, 1243/54
Source: Purchased from Jas. White

Gray-Milne Seismograph, 1885

Ewing Duplex Pendulum Seismograph, 1888
Height overall: 66 cm

Designed by Sir Alfred Ewing and made by the Cambridge Scientific Instrument Co. Horizontal ground motion is sensed by an inverted pendulum, free to move in any direction about its pivot, magnified by a connecting link, and scribed into a small smoked-glass plate on top of the case. The trace is not timed, but demonstrates the complex disturbance of the ground during an earthquake.

Inv. no. 1886-116   Neg. no. 2446/77
Source: Purchased from Cambridge Sci. Inst. Co

Ewing Duplex Pendulum Seismograph, 1888

Omori Horizontal Pendulum Seismograph, 1898
Frame height: 132 cm
Boom length: 122 cm

Fusakichi Omori designed various seismographs, this early example was made in Tokyo about 1898. The duplex pendulum consists of a boom 160 cm in length with a heavy lead mass enclosed in a nickel-plated cylinder; fine adjustments are made with the small inverted pendulum fixed below the mass. Movements of the boom are magnified through a linkage and registered by a glass stylus on a smoked-paper chart. A clock-driven stylus traces a time-datum with minute-marks. This seismograph registered earthquake shock waves and also slow and small ground movements.

Inv. no. 1928-279
Source: Presented by the Meteorological Office

Milne Horizontal-Pendulum Seismograph, 1899
Stand height overall: 55 cm
Boom length: 94 cm
See also: 1899–64, Seismogram (two earthquakes 1897), page 9.
1902–52, Seismogram (three earthquakes) 1901, page 9.

In 1895 John Milne designed the first horizontal-pendulum seismograph capable of detecting shockwaves from distant earthquakes. This instrument, No 24 of the series, made by R W Munro, improved on the original design and was adopted by the British Association as a standard observatory seismograph. The seismograph was made more sensitive by dispensing with the friction of linkage and pen-on-paper: it records photographically. Light from an oil lamp is reflected through a slit plate at the tip of the boom and falls across a second slit, cut at right-angles, in a panel on the recording apparatus. This beam, interrupted every hour by a clock-driven shutter, registers on a travelling sheet of photographic paper.

Inv. no. 1899-63   Neg. no. 297/56
Source: Purchased from R.W. Munro

Milne Lamp-post Seismograph, 1902
Boom length: 103 cm

John Milne built this seismograph at his observatory at Shide, Isle-of-Wight. The lamp-post was embedded in concrete and two horizontal pendulums were suspended at right-angles from its base. Each boom carried a lever system and glass stylus. The record was traced on smoked paper, with hourly timing marks.

Inv. no. 1932-517   Neg. no. 235/84
Source: Presented by Miss C Morey.

Milne Horizontal-Pendulum Seismograph, 1899

Milne Lamp-post Seismograph, 1902

Agamemnone Seismograph, 1907
Height overall: 114 cm

Invented by Professor Giovanni Agamemnone in 1907, this seismograph is unusual in having L-shaped pendulums, supported only by pivots. The pendulums are of iron tubing and carry disc weights of iron 25 cm in diameter. The arms are aligned N–S and E–W so that all components of horizontal ground movement are detected. Motion is transferred through aluminium levers to a stylus registering on a smoked paper chart; a second stylus, controlled electromagnetically, adds a time datum. Agamemnone seismographs were installed in observatories in Europe and North Africa. This example, made by Fascianelli of Rome, was maintained by Dr J E Crombie at Aberdeen.

Inv. no. 1933-74   Neg. nos. 793/53, 794/54
Source: Presented by the University of Aberdeen

Weichert Astatic Horizontal Seismograph, 1904
Height overall: 99 cm

This inverted pendulum seismograph was invented by Emil Weichert around 1904. The 1-metre pendulum consists of a heavy mass supported on a tapered column which is loosely coupled to a rigid framework by a system of Cardan springs and free to oscillate in two directions at right-angles. Two thrust-arms project from the mass in these directions and each is coupled through a series of aluminium levers to a light aluminium stylus. These two systems are coupled to damping pistons, stabilising the pendulum and magnifying the thrust-arm movements. The two records are scribed on a smoked paper chart. A solenoid lifts each stylus every minute to provide a time-mark. This seismograph was made by Spindler & Hoyer of Göttingen and used by the Meteorological Office.

Inv. no. 1928-280   Neg. nos. 295/56, 296/56
Source: Presented by the Meteorological Office

Milne Double-Boom Seismograph, 1908
Boom lengths: 91 and 92 cm

Two horizontal pendulums are carried at right-angles by the vertical pillar, their aluminium booms brought out parallel to each other. Both horizontal components of ground motion can thus be registered on one chart. For one component, the mass is not rigidly attached to the boom, but is balanced on a steel pivot, thereby reducing the effective moment of inertia of the pendulum. The seismograph can also be accurately tilted, to determine its static sensitiveness. The instrument registers photographically; its light source interrupted every hour to provide time-marks along the traces. This seismograph, made by R W Munro, was delivered to Eskdalemuir Observatory in 1908.

Inv. no. 1928–281   Neg. no. 1421/83/2
Source: Presented by the Meteorological Office

Milne Double-Boom Seismograph, 1908

Weichert Astatic Horizontal Seismograph, 1904

Milne Seismograph

No 9, made by R W Munro. Similar to 1899–63.

Inv. no. 1939-385
Source: Presented by the Meteorological Office

Mainka Horizontal Seismograph, 1912
Height overall: 178 cm

The pendulum mass consists of iron discs weighing altogether 440 kg; Mainka substituted a spring for the lower pivot and its distance from the centre of gravity is much less than in most other seismographs. A thrust-rod projecting from one side of the mass operates the damping system and magnifying levers. The recording stylus registers on a smoked paper chart and is raised every minute by an electromagnet, to provide time marks. This seismograph, made by J & A Bosch of Strassburg, was maintained by Dr J E Crombie of Aberdeen.

Inv. no. 1932-440   Neg. nos. 508/58, 509/58
Source: Dr J E Crombie

Galitzin Seismograph, 1910
Height overall of horizontal pendulum unit: 72 cm
See also: 1912–194, Seismogram (Turkestan 1911), page 9.
Neg. no. 292/66, Seismogram (Persia 1962)

Three pendulum units are set up, two at right-angles to detect horizontal motion and one to detect vertical motion. In each unit the boom ends carry induction coils which locate within the poles of a pair of magnets. Movement of the boom generates induction currents proportional to the displacement velocity. These currents are led through galvanometers whose mirrors reflect light beams onto a photographic chart. The boom movement can be magnified by a factor of 1000. All three components are recorded on one chart and are timed by electrical interruption of the traces. This seismograph, made by Hugo Masing of St Petersburg, was installed at Eskdalemuir Observatory in 1910 and transferred to Kew Observatory in 1925.

Inv. no. 1966-94
Source: Presented by the Meteorological Office

Milne-Shaw Seismograph, 1914
Height overall: 57 cm
Boom length: 47 cm
See also: 1952–123, Milne-Shaw seismograph, below.
1926–660 to 665 Seismograms, page 9.

Shaw modified Milne's seismograph to give magnification up to × 500 and he added magnetic damping. The apparatus is particularly sensitive to tilt and will register small changes of ground level in addition to responding to earthquake waves. The 19-inch boom carried a mass of 1 lb and is damped by an electrolytic copper vane floating between the poles of four tungsten steel magnets. A pivoted mirror on the boom reflects a light beam through a lens system onto the photographic chart. Magnification is thus partly mechanical and partly optical.

Inv. no. 1928-155   Neg. no. 7679
Source: Lent by the Board of Trade

Mainka Horizontal Seismograph, 1912

Milne-Shaw Seismograph, 1914
Similar to: 1928–155, Milne-Shaw seismograph.

Inv. no. 1952-123   Neg. no. 296/56
Source: Presented by the British Association for the Advancement of Science

Milne-Shaw Seismograph, 1914

Two Wood-Anderson Seismometers, 1933 and 1936
Height overall: 37 cm

Torsion suspension instruments were developed in California to record the short-period waves associated with local earthquakes. In these examples, constructed and tested at Kew Observatory between 1933 and 1965, fine wire suspends a copper block and mirror weighing together 3.15 g, between the poles of a damping magnet. The block hangs eccentrically and therefore responds to horizontal motion by turning on the wire. To record this motion, a light beam was focussed on this mirror and the reflection, magnified by distance of travel, registered on a photographic chart.

Inv. no. 1974-539   Neg. no. 415/84
Source: Presented by the Meteorological Office

Milne-Shaw Seismograph, 1935
Boom and stylus length: 186 cm

This seismograph, basically Shaw's adaptation of Milne's design, has been considerably altered over the years in order to run it within the Museum gallery. The boom, tied to a structural column of the building, carries a mass of 370 lbs in the form of disc weights. It is coupled to a stylus through an oil bath and paddle, and further stabilised by a magnetic field set up at the base of the stylus. A second stylus draws a time datum, marking each minute.

Inv. no. 1935-348   Neg. no. 306/84
Source: Purchased from J.J. Shaw

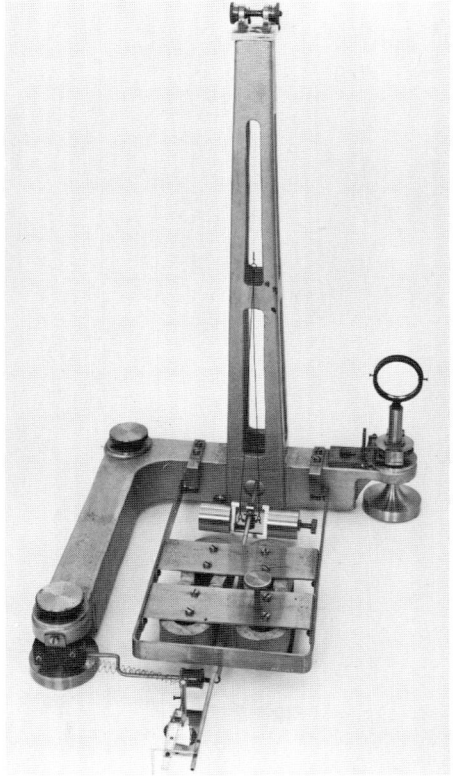

Milne-Shaw Seismograph, 1914

Kew Short-Period Vertical Seismograph, c1938
Length overall: 76 cm
See also 1966–94, Galitzin seismograph, and 1974–539, Two Wood-Anderson seismometers, above.

A direct-recording instrument with a magnification of 3000. Its purpose was to detect the short-period P-waves marking the onset of earthquakes. This apparatus was built in the Observatory workshops and from 1951 until 1969 operated in conjunction with Wood-Anderson and Galitzin seismometers.

Inv. no. 1974-541
Source: Presented by the Meteorological Office

Borehole Seismometer, 1980
Pendulum assembly weight: 4g
Size overall: 15 cm × 10 cm

The vertical-component unit of a set comprising three seismometers and feedback electronics. Fitted into a pressurised jacket 1 metre by 10 cm diameter, they are lowered down a borehole where they are free from the disturbing effects of temperature change and local vibration. The pendulums weigh only a few grams. Their movements are detected by a coil-and-magnet and telemetered by cable to the surface. The seismometers can be tuned to respond to various frequencies, according to their intended purpose.

Inv. no. 1980-1069   Neg. no. 295/84
Source: Dept. of Cybernetics, University of Reading

Wood-Anderson Seismometer, 1933

Milne-Shaw Seismograph, 1935

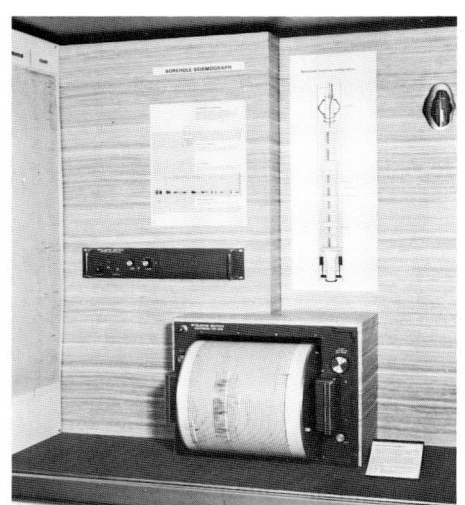

Borehole Seismometer, 1980

Perry Tromometer, demonstration model
Length overall: 41 cm

Designed by Professor John Perry to record the minor earth tremors which may precede large earthquake movements. The essential feature is a light spiral spring, made from strip metal, which turns through a wide angle in response to slight changes in length. One end of the spring is fixed; the other connects to the end of a balance-beam. With the beam unequally loaded, and the spring attached to the heavier arm, the apparatus acts as a recorder of vertical motion. The spring's rotation is observed directly by an attached pointer, or magnified by means of a spot of light reflected from an attached mirror.

Inv. no. 1937-155
Source: Oxford University Observatory

Milne-Macdonald Vibration Recorder, 1889
Length overall: 25 cm

Designed in Japan by John Milne to record vertical motion when no great magnification was required. The mass is cantilevered from a coiled spring and linked to a pencil tracing on a paper chart. This instrument was used to measure vibrations on railway tracks and within buildings during earthquakes, rather than the ground movement itself.

Inv. no. 1937-152   Neg. no. 344/75
Source: Oxford University Observatory

Milne-Macdonald Improved Vibration Recorder, 1889.
Length overall: 21 cm

John Macdonald, co-designer of these two vibration recorders, was a railway engineer in Japan. This instrument was primarily designed to record vertical vibrations in railway carriages and locomotives, and was also used to detect vibrations in buildings and other structures. The linkage between the adjustable mass and the recording pencil both magnifies the motion and damps the weight to make it practically dead-beat.

Inv. no. 1937-153   Neg. no. 345/75
Source: Oxford University Observatory

Milne Seismometer-Vibration Recorder, 1889.
Length overall: 32 cm

All three components are registered on this instrument, which was used in railway trains to measure vibrations on track or bridges, and on buildings during earthquakes. Magnification is limited but the chart speed could be varied as required for a detailed trace of the vibrations. This recorder was patented in Britain as No 6471 of 1889.

Inv. no. 1937-154   Neg. no. 452/59
Source: Oxford University Observatory

Milne-MacDonald Improved Vibration Recorder, 1889

Milne-MacDonald Vibration Recorder, 1889

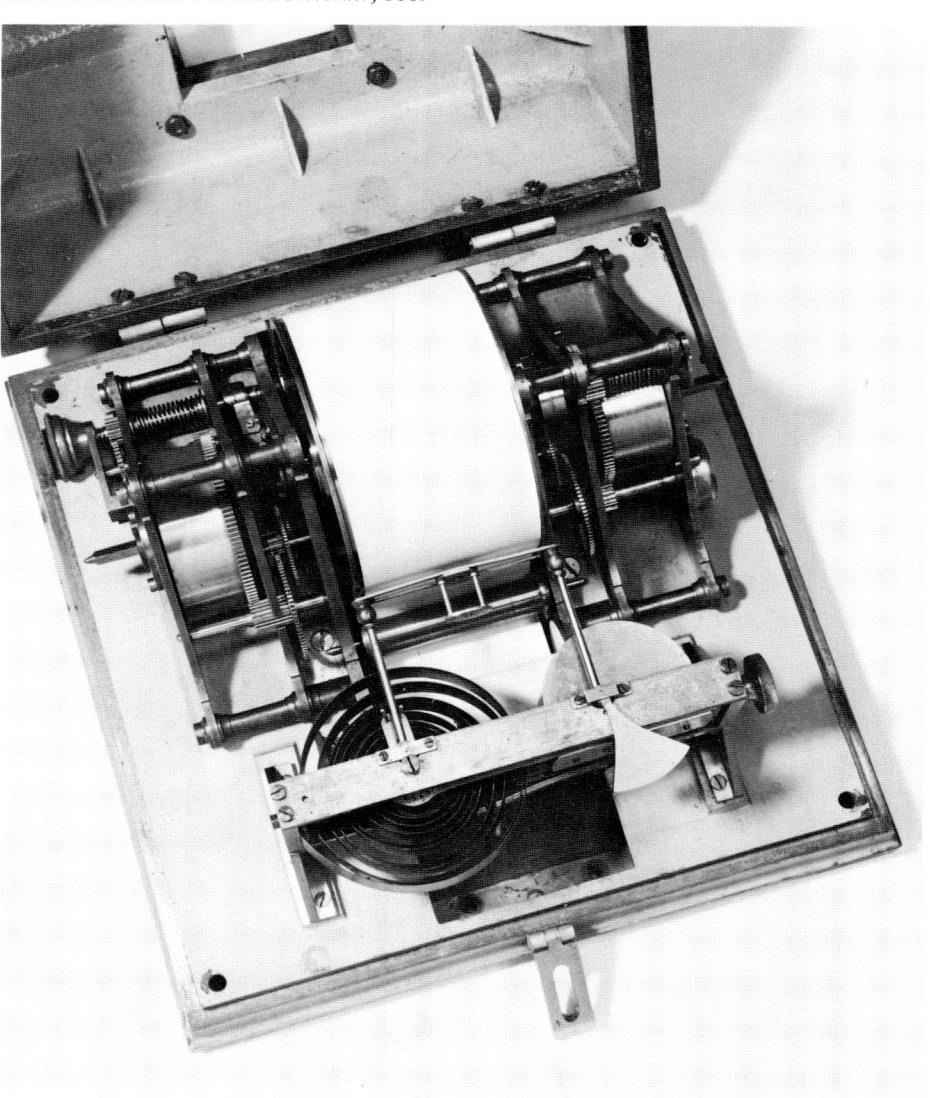

Seismograms

Tokyo earthquake, 15 Jan 1887, recorded on Ewing seismograph.
Inv. no. 1921-1055

Two earthquakes, 20 Sept 1897, recorded on Milne seismograph 1899–63 at Shide, I.O.W.
Inv. no. 1902-63

Three earthquakes, 9 Aug 1901, recorded on Milne seismograph, I.O.W.
Inv. no. 1902-52

Turkestan earthquake, 1911, recorded on Galitzin seismograph, Eskdalemuir.
Inv. no. 1912-194

Photo-enlargement, Puerto Rico earthquake, 11 Oct 1918, recorded at Shide, I.O.W.
Inv. no. 1926-661

Photo-enlargement, earthquake of 1 Oct 1922, recorded on Milne-Shaw seismograph at Hong Kong.
Inv. no. 1926-660

Annotated photo-enlargement, Yokohama earthquake, 1 Sept 1923, recorded at Oxford.
Inv. no. 1926-664   Neg. no. 65/54

Photo-enlargement, Tasmanian earthquake, 26 June 1924, recorded at Oxford.
Inv. no. 1926-663

Photo-enlargement, Atlantic Ocean earthquake, 13 Oct 1925, recorded at Cairo.
Inv. no. 1926-663

Photo-enlargement, two microseisms, recorded on Milne-Shaw seismographs in coalmines at Astley, Lancs.
Inv. no. 1926-665

Miscellaneous

Wire model showing motion of an earth particle during an earthquake.
90 × 43 cm.
Inv. no. 1889-25
Source: Purchased, Cambridge Sci. Inst. Co

Set of four Chinese postage stamps, 1953.
Includes one showing Chang Hêng seismometer.
Inv. no. 1976-312   Neg. no. 1018/76
Source: Transferred from Science Museum Library.

Porcelain figure of Chang Hêng (78–139AD)
50 cm high.
Inv. no. 1980-712
Source: Given by the Seismological Society of China

Book damaged in the Skopje earthquake, 26 July 1963.
Inv. no. 1964–96
Source: Presented, The British Council

Section 72″ relief globe showing the internal structure of the earth.
Inv. no. 1963-336   Neg. no. 728/66
Source: Purchased, George Philip & Son Ltd

Working model to illustrate vibrations of building structures.
Inv. no. 1978-593
Source: Thorpe Modelmakers/ScM Workshops

Miniature aseismic bearing pad.
As used to support buildings in earthquake-prone regions (15 cm square.)
Inv. no. 1979-637
Source: Presented by Spie-Batignolles BTP (France).

Atmospheric electricity

Cosmic radiation and radioactive matter make the air at all heights a slight conductor of electricity and even during fine weather there is a minute electric current flowing down from the air into the ground. Calculation shows that the air-earth current would within a few minutes neutralise the electric field which gives rise to it but for the action of a continuous compensating mechanism. The origin of the required supply current, for long a matter of doubt and controversy, is now thought to lie in rain-storms and thunderclouds, the negative charge carried to earth from the base of rainclouds and by lightning exceeding the positive charge carried to earth by falling rain.

As investigations into the nature of electricity proceeded during the 18th century it became apparent that there were resemblances between electric discharges and lightning flashes. In France Dalibard succeeded in 1752 in tapping via a conductor the current flowing from a thundercloud to earth and later the same year Benjamin Franklin succeeded by means of a kite in leading current from a cloud to a Leyden jar. Neither man tapped a lightning flash, which would have probably killed him, but they showed that the clouds were themselves electrically charged and that the lightning flash was probably a discharge of this static.

Franklin went on to propose that lightning conductors should be set up on buildings to attract the discharge and lead it harmlessly to earth. He made a conductor and set it up on his own house and by fixing a bell to it found that current flowed through it even when no storm was near. Argument raged throughout Europe as to whether lightning conductors did protect buildings but eventually it was conclusively shown that with careful construction, avoiding points of possible corrosion and earthing into a zone of permanently moist soil, such conductors did prevent damage. Wooden ships could also be protected from the hazards of lightning strikes, which were thought to be the cause of many ships being set on fire and being lost with all hands.

As telegraph and power transmission lines were set up across the country it became necessary to devise methods for preventing these excellent conductors becoming channels for lightning and passing the current along the line, which could lead to its damage, and in the case of telegraph lines, to injury to the operators. During the last century various devices were installed, such protectors or arresters being analagous to a fuse in the modern electrical wiring circuit.

Experiments with various forms of electrometer during the 18th and 19th centuries made it apparent that small changes occurred daily and seasonally in the earth's electric field in addition to the large changes associated with the overhead passage of thunderstorms. In 1843 Sir Francis Ronalds set up at Kew Observatory apparatus in which a 16-ft copper pipe protruding through the observatory roof led down to a table equipped with several types of electrometer. Sir William Thomson (later Lord Kelvin) also devised various electrometers for indoor and outdoor use and these were regularly used on scientific expeditions.

With such instruments it was possible to measure only the field at the earth's surface but eventually instruments were devised for attachment to sounding balloons in order to measure the charge within and above the clouds.

The sequence of flashes in a typical lightning discharge was revealed by photographs taken by C. V. Boys' high-speed lightning camera. Boys devised the camera in 1900 but did not get a successful photograph until 1928.

Kelvin Quadrant Electrometer, 1857

Electrometers

Volta Repulsion Electrometer, c 1845
Height overall: 60 cm

Potential difference causes the pith arms to diverge, the extent being read off against the scale. The flame of the insulated lamp reduces the lamp and other conducting material connected to it to the same potential as that of the nearby air.

Inv. no. 1957-108   Neg. no. 418/84
Source: Given by Kew Observatory

Peltier Repulsion Electrometer, 1848
Height overall: 24 cm

The light needle has a small magnet fixed across it at its pivot. The brass arms may be turned to come into contact with the needle. If a difference of potential exists, the needle will be deflected away from the magnetic meridian, the amount of deflection being measured against the scale.

Inv. no. 1884-57   Neg. no. 143
Source: Given by the GPO

Kelvin Absolute Electrometer, c 1870
Made by James White, Glasgow. No. 11
Height overall: 70 cm

The aluminium attracted disc is suspended above a fixed brass disc and maintained at a constant high potential. The fixed disc is put into contact with the body whose potential is to be measured. Attraction between the two discs is then balanced by means of a micrometer screw arrangement supporting the aluminium disc. The outer glass jar is covered with tinfoil to guard against leakage of the charges.

Inv. no. 1927-206
Source: Given by City and Guilds Institute, Gresham College, London

Kelvin Quadrant Electrometer, 1857
Made by Elliott Bros, London. No 1491
Height overall: 40 cm

The brass quadrants rest on a frame supported by glass pillars. In use one pair of the coupled quadrants is earthed, the other pair being connected to the body whose potential is to be measured. Within the quadrants an aluminium needle hangs at a zero position when the quadrants are at the same potential. Any difference in potential causes the needle to rotate; the amount of rotation is read off on the scale, by means of a telescope and a mirror attached to the needle suspension. A metal cage protects the instrument from disturbances arising from other nearby electrical apparatus.

Inv. no. 1926-284   Neg. no. 417/84
Source: Given by A.A. Campbell Swinton

Volta Repulsion Electrometer, c 1845   *Peltier Repulsion Electrometer, 1848*

Kelvin Portable Electrometers

Designed by Kelvin in 1867 and similar in principle to his absolute electrometer. The attracted disc, here a square, is placed at the bottom of the instrument, whose case forms the Leyden jar, connected with the gauge and guard plate. The scale is graduated by direct comparison with an absolute electrometer.

No 35, made by J. White, Glasgow, used on the national Antarctic expedition, 1901–4. Height overall 22 cm, height of electrometer 14 cm.
Inv. no. 1911-210   Neg. no. 416/84
Source: Given by the Admiralty Hydrographic Department

No 19, made by Kelvin & James White, Glasgow and London. Height 12 cm.
Inv. no. 1980-1875
Source: Given by the Meteorological Office

Kelvin Portable Electrometer, c 1900

Altielectrograph, c 1934

Devised by Dr F J Scrase at Kew Observatory for investigating electricity in and around thunderclouds. The electrograph was tied on a bamboo frame and sent aloft on a free balloon to heights around 8 km where it was detached, to return to earth on its own parachute.

Within the aluminium case a clock turns two recording discs. The lower is a smoked aluminium plate on which pressure and humidity traces are scribed by an aneroid and a hair hygrometer. The upper disc is insulated by ebonite fittings and records polarity changes. It carries pole-finding paper (impregnated with potassium ferrocyanide and ammonium nitrate) on which two iron electrodes bear. One electrode connects with the instrument frame, the other is led as a rubber-covered wire out of the case into the air. As the atmospheric charges reverse, a blue trace forms at whichever pin is carrying a positive charge.

Inv. no. 1962-66   Neg. no. 419/84
Source: Given by Dr F J Scrase

Altielectrograph, c 1934

Kelvin divided-ring and house electrometers
Height overall: 40 cm
Made by James White, Glasgow.

One half of the divided-ring is insulated, the other is connected to the instrument's metal case. A light aluminium needle is suspended horizontally by a fine glass fibre which also supports a stiff vertical wire from which a platinum wire dips into sulphuric acid contained in the bottom of the jar. A small mirror carried on this wire reflects a light beam from an external lamp. The Leyden jar is coated outside, and partially inside, with tinfoil. Platinum wire connects the tinfoil with the sulphuric acid. A metal cylinder fits into the Leyden jar, attached to a metal ring carried by its inner coating and extending above the level of the jar where the stiff wire for charging the instrument projects.

This electrometer was installed at Kew Observatory in 1861, to measure potential difference in the atmosphere in connection with a photographic recording apparatus.

Height overall: 33 cm
Made by James White, Glasgow

The house electrometer measures differences of potential between two conducting systems: the one consisting of the aluminium needle, repelling plate and inner coating of the jar, the other being the insulating cage. This apparatus is now damaged and incomplete.

Inv. no. 1876-787
Source: Given by the Kew Observatory

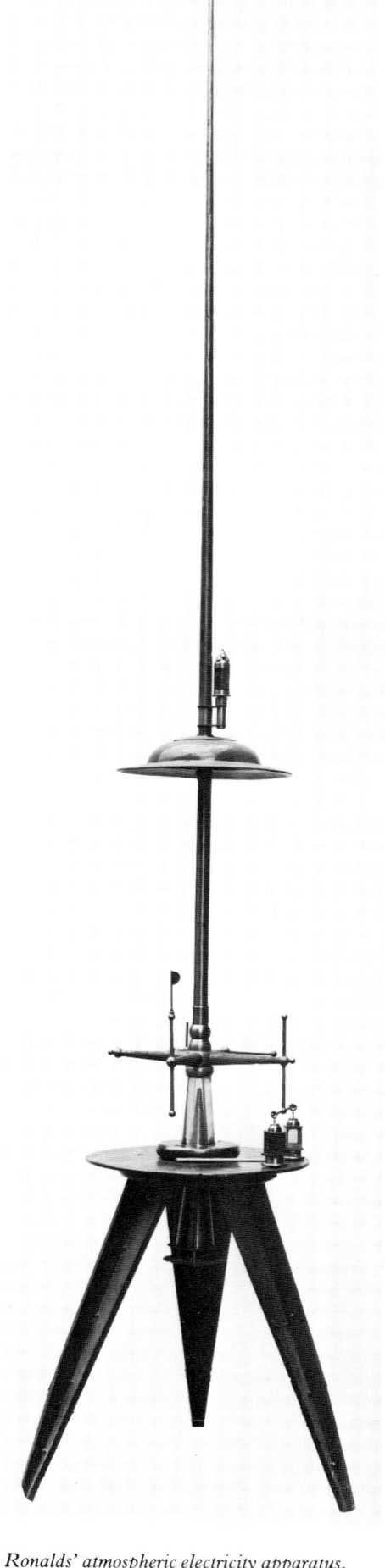

Ronalds' atmospheric electricity apparatus, 1843

Ronalds' atmospheric electricity apparatus, 1843

The principal conductor, a copper tube originally 4.9 m high, projected through the Observatory roof and carried a lamp enclosed in a Volta collecting lantern. At the base of the tube is a hollow glass cone, which was kept dry by a copper funnel passing up its interior and continuously heated by a small lamp. Attached to the cross-arms below the collecting tube are gold leaf, Henley and straw electroscopes which registered the variations. Regular observations were made at Kew with this apparatus for several years, using different electroscopes.

Inv. no. 1876-792   Neg. no. 3932
Source: Given by Kew Observatory

Electric alarm bells, 1862
See also: 1939-194, Replica of Franklin's lightning conductor, page 14.

Benjamin Franklin had devised this alarm system in 1752 to give warning of atmospheric electricity currents flowing through his lightning conductor. The outer bells connect to the conductor; the central one to earth. Current discharges to earth passing through the intermediate balls, and vibrating them against the bells, so ringing the alarm.

Inv. no. 1862-71
Source: Given by the Belgian Government

Miscellaneous

29 spectrum tubes of gases from aerolites.
Inv. no. 1923-369
Source: Lent by the Institute of Electrical Engineers

Photograph, Boys' lightning camera, 1934 with fixed lenses and moving drum.
Inv. no. 1935-586
Source: Given by Sir Charles Boys

Records of atmospheric electricity

a) Positive potential gradient, Kew Observatory, 1909–10
b) Positive gradient with occasional negative excursions, Kew Observatory, 1909–10
c) Records with water-dropper and Dole-Zalek electrometers, Eskdale Observatory, 1910.
Inv. nos. 1912-185, 1912-186, 1912-187
Source: Lent by the Meteorological Office

Telegraph Line Protectors

In some forms of protector the lightning discharge could be made to jump a gap between plates or wires, one of which was connected to the telegraph line and the other led to earth. Another form involved laying a fusible wire into the circuit. A strong discharge melted the wire, allowing the current an alternative path to earth.

Russian fusible line protector, c 1876
On base 9 cm diam.

Placed in circuit, fine wire holds a brass lever against a spring. When lightning strikes the line, the wire fuses and the lever is pushed onto an earth terminal. Air gap protectors are also provided.

Inv. no. 1876-1345
Source: Lent by the General Director of Russian Telegraphs

GPO serrated plate protector, c 1878
On base 10 cm long

Sir C W Siemens originated this type in 1860. Two corrugated tinned brass plates are separated by paper.

Inv. no. 1915-210
Source: Given by the GPO

GPO bobbin protector, c 1880
On base 11 × 17 cm

A brass tube is connected to earth. The line wires are led to terminals inside the tube, spaced by an air gap.

Inv. no. 1888-223
Source: Given by the GPO

Varley's globe protector, 1861
On base 20 × 20 cm.

Four platform wires connected to the telegraph line are arranged with points close to a horizontal earthed wire, the whole assembly contained in a vacuum within a glass globe.

Inv. no. 1913-251   Neg. no. 421/84
Source: Given by the GPO

GPO serrated plate protector, c 1876
On base 27 × 13 cm

The plates are connected alternately to the line and to earth. A strong current will jump the gaps and be led to earth instead of flowing along the line.

Inv. no. 1876-1332   Neg. no. 420/84
Source: Given by the GPO

GPO comb protector
On base 16 × 12 cm

Three toothed plates, the centre led to earth and the outer pair to the line wires.

Inv. no. 1915-219
Source: Given by the GPO

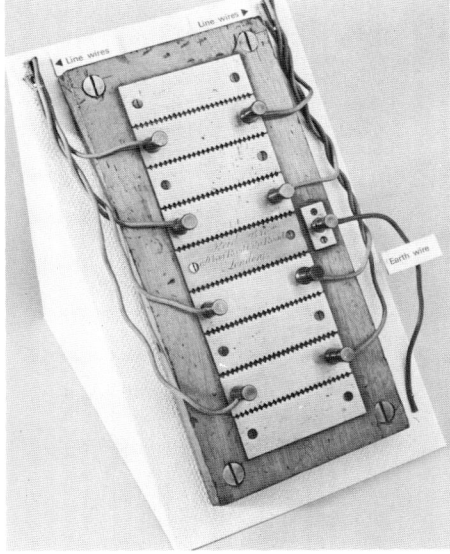
GPO serrated plate protector, c 1876

Varley's globe protector, 1861

Lightning Conductors for Buildings

Replica of one of the earliest conductors erected by Benjamin Franklin in America, c 1749.
See also 1862-71, Electric alarm bells, page 13.
Inv. no. 1939-194   Neg. no. 144/56
Source: Purchased from the Franklin Institute

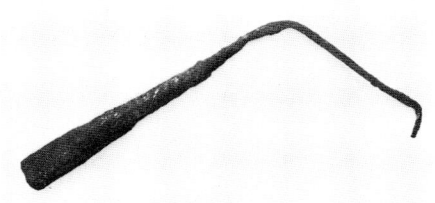

Replica of Franklin's conductor, c 1749

Section of lightning conductor from St Paul's Cathedral, c 1770.
See also 1907-58, terminal aigrette, below.
A system of lightning protection was fitted on the recommendation of a Royal Society committee. The conductor consisted mainly of lengths of wrought-iron bar with overlapping joints. (A century later, corrosion and breakage having destroyed its effectiveness, it was replaced by copper rope conductors).
Inv. no. 1907-57
Source: Lent by Killingworth Hedges

Terminal aigrette, c 1876, struck by lightning.
The central spike passes through a copper ball into which are screwed the three secondary points.
Inv. no. 1916-60
Source: Presented by R C Cotting & Co

Spratt's patent woven conductor.
Follows Spratt's 1860 patent but in these later versions the transverse wires of zinc have been replaced by copper. Both inventory items comprise new and damaged specimens.
Inv. no. 1893-131; 1921-46
Sources: Lent by J G Symons; Given by Killingworth Hedges

Copper tape and 4-way copper joint, c 1880
Inv. no. 1913-535
Source: Lent by Killingworth Hedges

Terminal aigrette and elevator, 1899.
See also 1907-57, part of St Paul's Cathedral conductor, c 1770, above.
Contains features of the 'Air to Earth' system patented by Killingworth Hedges in 1899. A conductor of this type was fitted on St Paul's Cathedral in 1900. The copper conductor continues as the central point of the aigrette. It is in good contact with a collar holding other rods, the whole being filled with solder.
Inv. no. 1907-58
Source: Lent by Killingworth Hedges

Hedges horizontal conductor, 1901, fitted on a roof tile.
Inv. no. 1915-28
Source: Lent by Killingworth Hedges

Air terminal with grooved lead joint as used to secure horizontal conductors, 1905.
Inv. no. 1918-3
Source: Lent by Killingworth Hedges

Terminal aigrette damaged by lightning in 1913.
A 4-point Hedges terminal.
Inv. no. 1914-691
Source: Given by Killingworth Hedges

Two rainwater pipes bonded for use as lightning conductors, c 1910.
Lead plugs are clamped against the pipes whilst a heavy stranded cable across the pipe joints ensures good electrical connection.
Inv. no. 1921-38
Source: Given by Killingworth Hedges

Set of miniature lightning conductor fittings, 1977.
Displayed on a model house.
Inv. no. 1977-647
Source: Given by W J Furse & Co

Miscellaneous

Specimens of wires etc struck by lightning

14 fulgurites (sand fused by lightning discharge).
Inv. no. 1921-427
Source: Given by Killingworth Hedges

4 portions of lead flashing from a roof, damaged by lightning.
Inv. no. 1921-41
Source: Given by Killingworth Hedges

1 piece of signal wire, 1 piece of earth wire from a telegraph block instrument damaged when lightning struck the line, 1902.
Inv. no. 1921-39
Source: Given by Killingworth Hedges

Glazed box of overhead line wire samples struck by lightning.
Inv. no. 1923-381
Source: Lent by the Institution of Electrical Engineers

Rhé electrometer, 1875
Magnet length 8 cm

Designed by Professor Melsens to measure the strength of discharges between air and ground.
The electrometer is connected to a lightning conductor or a telegraph line earth wire. It consists of a coil of wire with a magnetic needle supported across it laying N–S. An iron bar slides into the coil, aligned E–W. When current passes, the bar becomes magnetised and deflects the needle. This deflection varies with the intensity of current and is measured against a degree scale marked on a card between the needle and the coil. A card and stage allow the elevation of the magnet for table experiments.

Inv. nos. 1876-865, 1876-866
Source: Lent by Dr. Mann

Magnetic links and holder, 1951

Used to record the direction and peak value of the large currents that flow to earth when an overhead power line is struck by lightning.
The links consist of several strips of cobalt steel enclosed in a 6 cm long plastic tube. The holder, normally of oak, is here made of perspex for exhibition purposes.
When the conductor is struck the links become magnetised. Subsequent laboratory measurement of their remanent magnetism supplies information on the nature of the discharge current.

Inv. no. 1952-385
Source: Given by the British Electricity Authority

Boys' original lightning camera, 1900
Camera box: 30 × 20 × 26 cm

Sir Charles Boys built this camera to check his theory that a lightning flash consisted of rapid strokes along the same path. It has a fixed photographic plate and two identical lenses mounted on a disc which is turned by hand through suitable gearing. As the discharge proceeds, the moving lenses form images of the separate strokes on different parts of the plate.

Inv. no. 1937-559 Neg. no. 36/54
Source: Given by Sir Charles Boys

Boys' original lightning camera, 1900

Brontometer, 1890
Made by Richard Frères, Paris
Size overall: 58 × 58 cm × 125 cm high

Apparatus devised by G J Symons to register thunderstorm phenomena. Seven pens record simultaneously on a 12-inch paper chart driven at 1:2 inches per minute, as follows:
  a) Time-datum, readable to one second.
  b) Wind-speed from a Richard anemometer.
  c) Intensity of rainfall, estimated by observer.
  d) Lightning flashes, as observed.
  e) Audibility of thunder, as observed.
  f) Intensity of hail, estimated by observer.
  g) Atmospheric pressure variation.

Only a, b, and g, operate automatically, other data are registered directly by the observer. A galvanised iron tank in the insulated cabinet under the apparatus acted as a reservoir to a series of aneroid capsules above. The pressure record was therefore of relative, not absolute, values. (The iron tank is now missing).

Inv. no. 1935-203 Neg. no. 489/84
Source: Lent by the Royal Meteorological Society

Brontometer, 1890

Gravity

The force of gravity (g) is a fundamental quantity in physics. The intensity of gravity determines the weight of the standard kilogram and allows us to calculate the sizes and masses of the heavenly bodies. Gravity also controls the rate of a swinging pendulum which consequently has been used to measure both the absolute intensity and regional variations in gravity.

According to the type of survey being made, different geophysical pendulums are used. The *simple pendulum*, a weight suspended by cord or wire from a fixed support, was soon replaced by more accurate types. The *invariable pendulum* has a fixed knife edge near one end and a heavy weight at the other. It is used solely to compare the gravitational force at different places and it must be swung in a vacuum or have the observed results corrected for the effects of atmospheric friction.

A *convertible pendulum* has a fixed knife edge near each end, a fixed and heavy weight at one end, and a movable, lighter weight at the other. The light weight is adjusted so that the period of swing is the same from each knife edge, no correction for friction being required. This type is also effectively a *seconds pendulum*, one whose length measured between the point of suspension and the centre of mass is such that each beat occupies one second. This length is approximately one metre but, being proportional to the force of gravity, will vary in different parts of the globe and it is therefore able to measure the oblateness of the earth. Half-second and quarter-second pendulums are also made. *Detached pendulums* swing under the influence of gravity alone; *attached pendulums* may be driven by clockwork to maintain the swings.

Henry Kater was the first person to design, construct and use a compound pendulum to measure the absolute intensity of gravity, in London, during 1817–18. Thereafter, observations were made in other parts of the world, increasing accuracy being achieved by swinging the pendulum within a vacuum chamber.

Faced with the difficulties of transporting and setting up such cumbersome apparatus, von Sterneck developed, in 1880, a shorter pendulum, timed by electrical signals. Vening Meinesz used similar apparatus, from 1923 onwards, in a submarine, to measure the variation of gravity across the oceans.

Another type of experiment, to determine the universal constant of gravitation (G), can be undertaken in the laboratory. A large mass – for example, a lead sphere – is placed so as to attract a small suspended body, and this attraction is measured and compared with that of the whole earth upon the same body. Henry Cavendish carried out a successful experiment of this type in 1797–8 by means of a torsion balance. C V Boys, using quartz fibres which were more elastic than Cavendish's metal wire, obtained more accurate results with his apparatus between 1889 and 1894.

The general increase in gravitational attraction away from the equator showed that the earth was not a perfect sphere but was slightly flattened at the poles. Increasingly accurate measurements on land and at sea revealed variations in deep rock density beneath mountain ranges, plains and oceans which were subsequently interpreted in terms of crustal evolution and subduction: modern plate tectonics theories are built on this data. More detailed information is now obtained by miniature gravimeters carried overland, set on the sea bed, or flown in aircraft and satellites.

Pendulum Apparatus

Two Invariable Clock Pendulums, c 1750

Made by Shelton, who supplied the Royal Society with various timekeepers for the Transit of Venus and other expeditions. Each pendulum is cast in one piece of brass. Both consist of cylindrical rods terminating in disc-shaped bobs. One has knife-edge suspension, the other hangs on a spring.

The pendulum with knife-edge suspension was taken on John Ross's Arctic Expedition of 1818 and swung as a seconds pendulum to measure gravity. Sir Edward Sabine also used it subsequently for gravity measurements.

Inv. no. 1902-146
Source: Lent by the Royal Society

Kater's Convertible Pendulum, 1817
See also: 1900-131 Telescope used by Kater, page 21.

The rod is a plate brass bar, 1.5 × 0.125 inches, with two triangular holes 39.4 inches apart to admit the knife-edges. The cylindrical weight is fixed to the bar; a second sliding weight near the other end is fixed at any point by two screws. A third adjustable slide weight can be moved near the centre of the bar, over a scale showing its precise position. Originally the bar carried brass, deal, and whalebone pointer extensions beyond the knife edges.

Kater used this pendulum to find the length of a pendulum vibrating seconds in the latitude of London in 1817. It was straightened and reground in 1873 and fitted with brass tailpieces for Heaviside to repeat Kater's experiments at Kew during 1873–4.

Inv. no. 1902-144   Neg. no. 577/61
Source: Lent by the Royal Society

Invariable Pendulum, 1818
See also: 1902-143 Two thermometers, page 21.

The 5-foot brass bar is 1.6 × 0.125 inches thick and carries a flat circular sliding weight, below which it is reduced to 0.7 inches wide and painted black for easy comparison with a clock pendulum. In use the pendulum swung on wootz steel knife-edges resting on agate planes, the whole assembly firmly held in a massive iron frame.

This pendulum was used by Henry Kater during 1818–19 to measure the length of a seconds pendulum at the principal stations of the Trigonometrical Survey of Great Britain.

Inv. no. 1902-145   Neg. no. 574/61
Source: Lent by the Royal Society

Boxed set of two invariable pendulums with agate planes and dummy

Inv. no. 1914-583, 584, 585
Source: Lent by the Royal Society

Invariable Pendulum No 11 with agate plane, 1827

Made by Thomas Jones and similar in size to No 10 (Inv. no. 1914-587). Swung by Henry Foster in 1828–31, by Francis Baily in 1831, 1833 and 1840, by Thomas Maclear in 1839. It was then lent to the Admiralty for some years, returned to Kew, swung by John Herschel in 1881, lent to the US Coast and Geodetic Survey for a world voyage in 1882–4 and finally employed in 1888–89 to compare the length of a seconds pendulum at Kew and at Greenwich.

In 1833 Baily modified it as he had done No 10: rounding the knife-edges and planes, cleaning the pendulum and making two holes in it near the knife-edges.

Inv. no. 1914-586   Neg. no. 576/61
Source: Given by the Meteorological Office

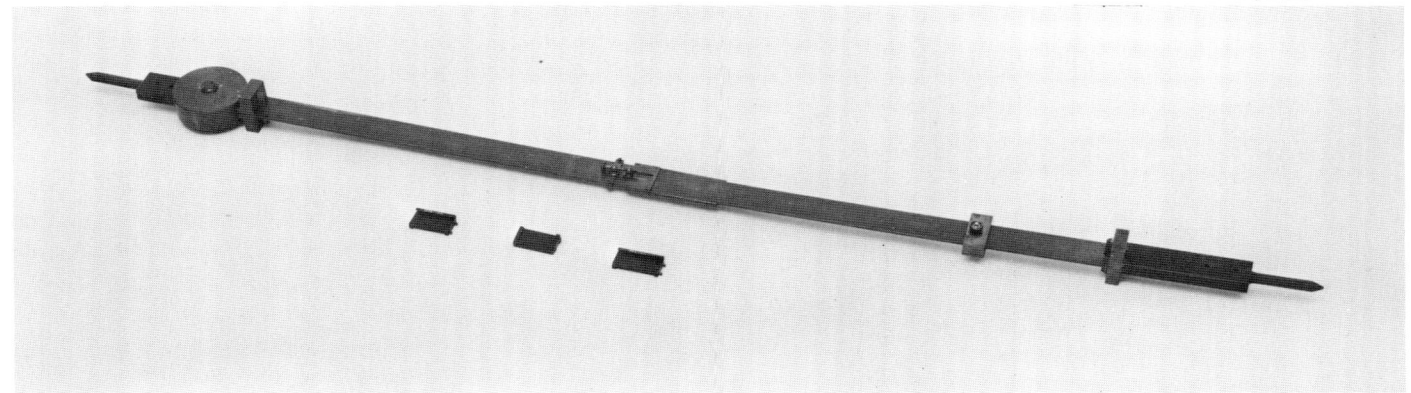

Kater's Convertible Pendulum, 1817

Invariable Pendulum, 1818

Invariable Pendulum No 10 with agate planes and accessories, 1827

Made by Thomas Jones; the 5-foot bar is 1¾ × ⅛ inches. The observing telescope is mounted to slide laterally on a short graduated horizontal bar and can also move vertically and in azimuth.

Henry Foster took this pendulum on his Atlantic voyage of 1828–31. Baily swung it in 1831 and 1834, modifying it in 1833 (see No 11). It was taken by Lt Murphy on the Euphrates Expedition of 1835–36 and went with James Ross to the Antarctic in 1839.

Inv. no. 1914-587   Neg. no. 575/61
Source: Given by the Meteorological Office

Invariable Pendulum No 8, 1826

Made by Thomas Jones. A plate brass bar 1.75 × 0.125 inches and about 5 foot long including the tailpiece. Wootz knife edges are supported on agate planes.

In 1826–27 Sabine used it to determine the length of the seconds pendulum in London and in Paris.

Inv. no. 1902-142   Neg. no. 578/61
Source: Lent by the Royal Society

Kew Vacuum Apparatus, 1828

See also: 1900-131, Telescope used by Kater
1902-143, Two thermometers by Jones, page 21.

A Kater convertible pendulum is housed in vacuum apparatus originally constructed c 1828, designed to eliminate friction as the pendulum swings. The agate planes are firmly supported on a slate bed. The vacuum chamber consists of an iron base with viewing windows, surmounted by three glass cylindrical sections. A dummy pendulum with two thermometers was hung in front of the operative one.

In its present form the apparatus was installed at Kew to test pendulums sent out for the Great Trigonometrical Survey of India between 1865 and 1873.

Inv. no. 1914-589
Source: Given by the Meteorological Office

Pendulum by Baily, RAS No 2

Inv. no. 1939-388   Neg. nos. 372/62, 373/62
Source: Given by the Meteorological Office

Gravity Pendulum Apparatus, c 1865

A sturdy knock-down wooden frame supports a copper chamber in which the pendulum can be swung under vacuum. The observer views the pendulum through glass panels, to compare its rate of swing with a pendulum clock standing behind it.

This apparatus was sent to India in 1865 and used until 1872 for a series of gravity measurements taken from the Himalayas to the far south of the country, as part of the Great Trigonometrical Survey.

Inv. nos. 1914-588, 1914-590, 1914-593
Neg. no. 1085/82
Source: Given by the Meteorological Office

Pendulum by Baily, RAS No 2

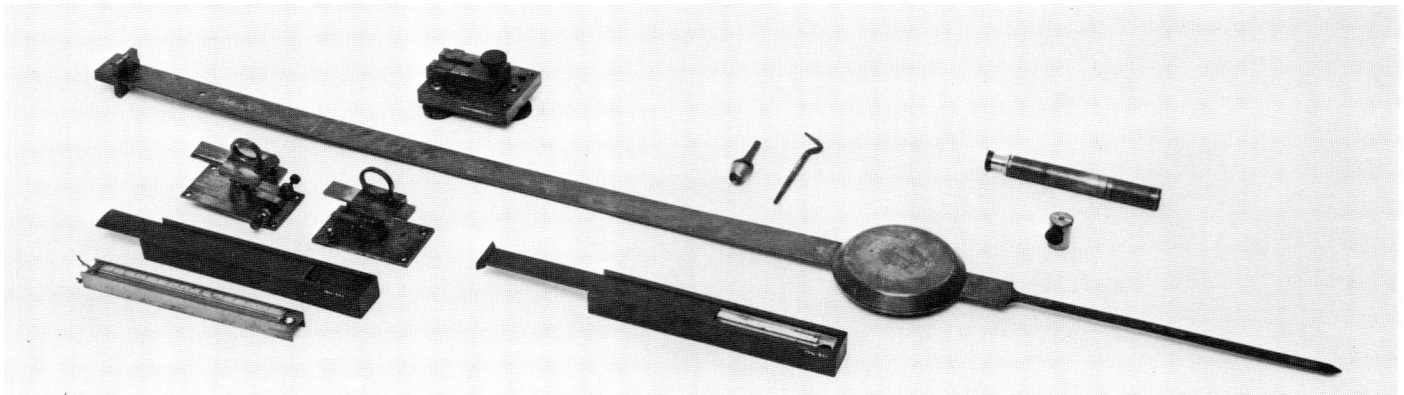

Invariable Pendulum No 10, 1827

Invariable Pendulum No 8, 1826

Gravity Pendulum Apparatus, c 1865

Von Sterneck Pendulum Apparatus, 1900

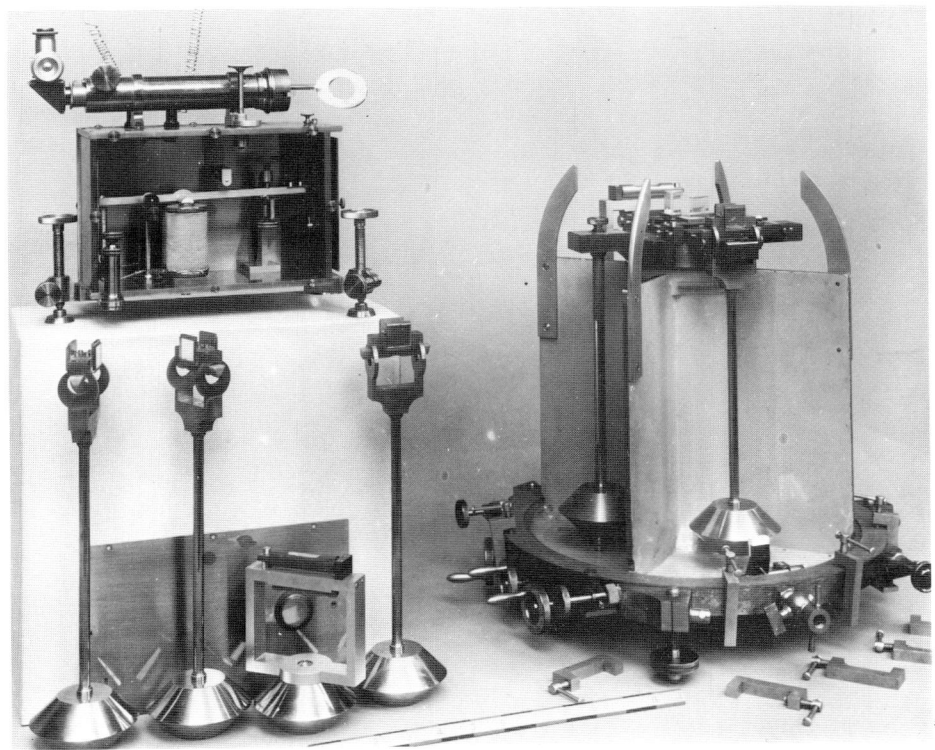

Von Sterneck Pendulum Apparatus by Stuckrath, 1900, with clock

A modified version of the apparatus developed by von Sterneck in 1882–85 to investigate the variation of gravity within deep mines. Three 25-cm pendulums, together with a dummy pendulum carrying a thermometer, fit under an airtight casing. The adjacent box contains flash apparatus for observing coincidences between the pendulum and a chronometer. An electromagnet in circuit with the chronometer moves a shutter at the end of each second, throwing a flash of light onto the pendulum mirror. The apparent position of the reflected flash depends on the position of the pendulum at the instant of reflection. The pendulums are controlled from outside the casing, the thermometer and mirrors being observed through windows.

This apparatus was used on the British Antarctic Expedition of 1901–4, on the Egyptian Survey of 1909–13, and in Greenland in 1926.

Inv. nos. 1900-115, 1900-116
Neg. nos. 118, 119
Source: Purchased from the maker

Two Holweck-Lejay Dynamic Gravimeters, 1934

The inverted pendulum, a fused quartz rod about 6×0.4cm diameter, is driven by a combination of gravity and the elastic restoring force of an elinvar spring. The period is varied by an adjustable quartz ring sliding on the rod. Electrostatic action is eliminated by coating the quartz with platinum and surrounding the whole by a Faraday cage. The pendulum is observed by a microscope focussed on a fine quartz thread at the upper end of the rod. A thermometer is set in the metal frame, the entire apparatus being sealed inside a glass cover. Dynamic gravimeters can only be used over the small range of values for which they are adjusted; they are subject to errors in levelling and to ground vibration, hence are unsuited to observations at sea. In the right circumstances however, they are more accurate than invariable pendulums.

Inv. nos. 1953-221, 1953-222
Source: Lent by Imperial College

Torsion apparatus

Baily's Torsion Apparatus, 1841

The apparatus is in poor condition and incomplete, consisting now of the long foil-lined mahogany box with glazed ends, (which housed the deal balance rod), and an upright column for the suspension wires. A fitted box contains 24 small lead, ivory and brass balls, wires and small fittings. Other brass parts used in these tests have recently been found.

Francis Baily made an extensive series of observations in 1841–42 at the request of the Royal Astronomical Society.

Inv. no. 1908-95
Source: Given by the Royal Astronomical Society

Boys' Original Torsion Balance, 1889
See also: Neg. no. 376/59 Sectional diagram of this balance.

After discovering how to produce quartz fibres, which are more responsive to torsion than metal wire, Professor C V Boys designed this miniature torsion balance for experiments to measure the gravitational constant. The small masses are lead cylinders 11.3 × 3mm diameter, attached by light brass arms to a glass tube suspended from the quartz fibre which carries a mirror. The large masses are lead cylinders 50.8mm in length and diameter attached inside the large brass tube which rotates on the base. The scales and observing telescope were set up 10.5m and 3.6m respectively from the mirror.

Boys first demonstrated the apparatus at the Royal Institution and at the BAAS meeting in Leeds. He was able to make it respond to 1 part in 2000 of the force, a considerable improvement over the 1:100 sensitivity of earlier torsion balances.

Inv. no. 1931-942   Neg. no. 1064/73
Source: Given by Prof. C V Boys FRS

Boys' Torsion Balance, 1889, by Cambridge Sci. Inst. Co

Based on Boys' original design, the light weights are two gold balls hung by quartz fibres from the ends of a beam mirror which itself is carried by a single quartz thread from the torsion head. The heavy attracting masses hang on phosphor-bronze wires from heads of pillars in the lid of the apparatus. There are sets of gold weights of 0.2 and 0.25 inches diameter and cylinders of 0.25 inches length and diameter. The lead weights are 2.25 and 4.25 inches diameters. A scale of 4800 divisions of nearly 0.5mm each is set up 7m from the mirror and read by telescope. Movements of 0.025mm, equal to an angle of 0.66 seconds of arc, can be read.

Inv. no. 1891-99
Source: Purchased from the maker

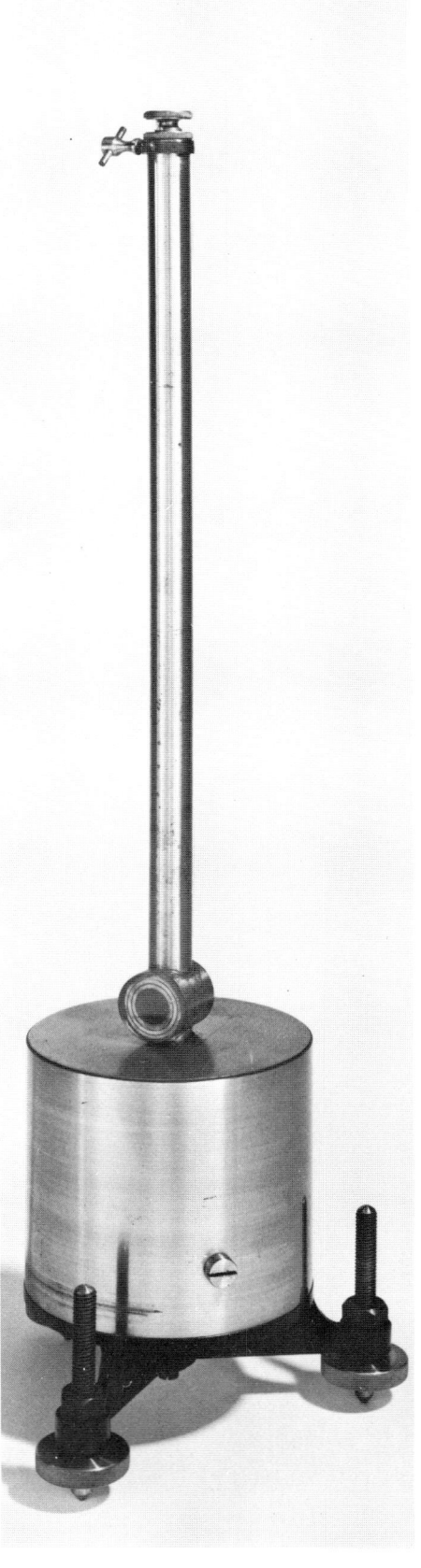

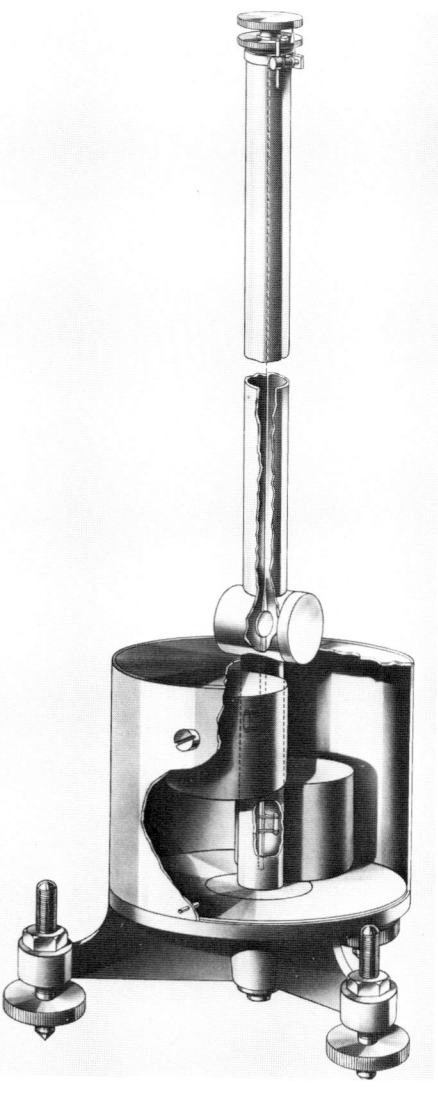

Boys' Original Torsion Balance, 1889   *Boys' Original Torsion Balance, 1889: construction*

Miscellaneous

Henry Cavendish's Laboratory and Torsion Balance, 1798
Scale model 1:48

Reconstruction based on the description in *Philosophical Transactions*, 1798.

Inv. no. 1977-417
Source: Science Museum Workshops

Telescope

Used by Kater for pendulum observations.

Inv. no. 1900-131
Source: Lent by the Royal Society

Two Thermometers, 1818

Made by Thomas Jones; one graduated $-8°F$ to $175°F$ and $-27°R$ to $95°R$, the other $7°F$ to $150°F$ and $-17°R$ to $78°R$. Used for pendulum experiments on John Ross's 1818 Arctic Expedition and others.

Inv. no. 1902-143
Source: Lent by the Royal Society

Photograph of Poynting's Balance, 1878

Professor J H Poynting used this balance by Oertling to determine the mean density of the earth and the gravitational constant.

Inv. no. 1921-31
Source: Given by the National Physical Laboratory

Dutch Geodetic Commission Marine Gravity Surveys, 1923–32

Map showing track of submarine K2, 1923.
Inv. no. 1924-712
Source: Purchased from the Dutch Geodetic Commission

Two photographs of pendulum apparatus.
Inv. no. 1924-716
Source: Purchased from the Dutch Geodetic Commission

Three gravity records made at sea in 1923.
Inv. no. 1935-476
Source: Given by Dr F A Vening Meinesz

Chart showing Meinesz' gravity profiles across the Atlantic and Pacific, 1926.
Inv. no. 1928-136
Source: Given by the Royal Geographic Society

Three gravity records made at sea in 1932 by Meinesz.
Inv. no. 1935-477
Source: Given by Dr F A Vening Meinesz

Tide measurement

Knowledge of the range of tide at any given place is vital for navigators, fishermen working shallow waters and for engineers constructing docks and harbours. For these purposes the range could be measured by means of simple marked poles affixed to a wall or jetty. For the more accurate records needed for analysis and prediction continuously recording apparatus was designed. Readings on exposed staff gauges were affected by the height of the waves and by the wind so one of the first steps taken was to measure the height of the water, not in the open sea, but in a well filled by the sea in which water-level did not fluctuate with each wave but rose and fell smoothly with the tide.

The first self-recording tide gauge was probably that devised by Henry Palmer for use at London Dock in 1831. He built a shaft open at the bottom to the river so that his float moved up and down with the tide. This float was connected to a counterbalance by a chain which wound around a barrel. The vertical movement of the chain was transformed by the barrel into a rotary one which by means of shafts and gear wheels was transferred to a rack carrying a steel writing pencil. The pencil drew a scaled-down water-level curve on graph paper secured on a drum moved by clockwork.

By the 1850s recording float gauges working on principles similar to those of Palmer had been set up at major ports in Britain and abroad. Apart from their regular records, ships on voyages of exploration had for many years been measuring tidal range and the solar time of high and low water of various points on their voyages. From all these records William Whewell drew the first chart attempting to show world co-tidal lines, which he published in 1833 in the Royal Society's *Philosophical Transactions*.

The installation of a tide gauge on the shore presents little difficulty but the measurement of tides in the open sea was not so easily accomplished. As the water rises at high tide, pressure is increased at the sea bed, so most of these early instruments were pressure recorders, like an aneroid barometer, with a Bourdon tube as sensor. They were anchored on the sea bed and buoyed for easy recovery. One of the first was that of Favé, devised in 1887. Another, that of Mensing, first constructed around 1893, was basically a differential manometer. Both these instruments were modified and improved in the early part of this century and were in regular use.

Tide analysis and prediction

The complete tidal curve of heights at any place is the sum of a number of oscillations of varying periods each corresponding to the cycle of an astronomical disturbing force. Such a record curve may be analysed into its components and it is then possible to recompute these for the future and thus predict for any given place the tidal range and water height at any given time.

Tide Gauges

Recording Tide Gauge, 1850
Made by John English, Newcastle on Tyne
Height overall: 75 cm

The large wheel carries the float line. A counterweight turns over a smaller coaxial wheel. This wheel system is geared to a pointer to indicate the height of water at any moment. At the same time, through a rack and pinion mechanism, it draws a trace onto a horizontal rotating drum. A range of 12 feet above and below the mean position is allowed for. This tide gauge was used for many years at Lowestoft Harbour.

Inv. no. 1926-775   Neg. no. 578/76
Source: Lent by the London and N E Railway Co

Recording Tide Gauge, 1850

Légé's Improved Portable Tide Gauge, 1881

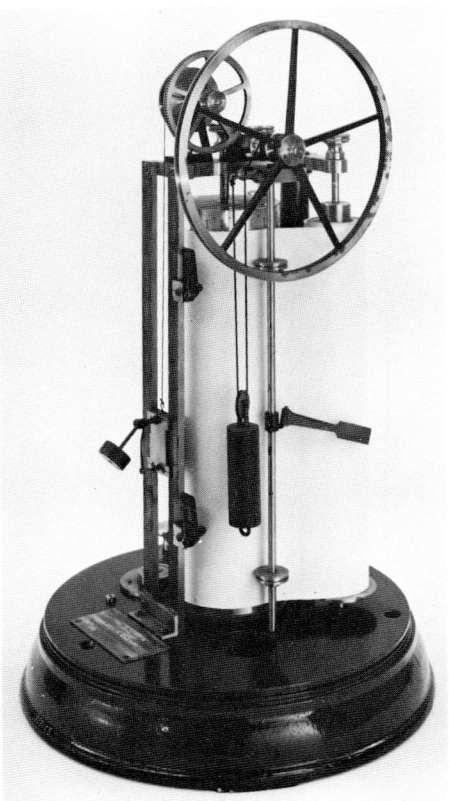

Légé's Improved Portable Tide Gauge, 1881
Made by A Légé & Co, London
Recorder height: 55 cm, float diameter: 11 cm

Vertical storage rollers carry one month's supply of plain paper. It passes round a clockwork-driven drum at ¾ inch per hour. Pins around the top and bottom of the drum puncture the chart to provide hourly and 24-hourly time-marks. One or more stationary pencils can be attached to draw fixed datum lines. The float wire passes over a reducing pulley and is attached to a pencil holder sliding between two brass guides engraved with a range scale.

Inv. no. 1922-45   Neg. no. 1120/76
Source: Purchased

US Coast & Geodetic Survey Tide Gauge, c 1924
Made by Bausch & Lomb, No 11681
Recorder height: 25 cm, float diameter: 8.5 cm

A simple lightweight apparatus designed for field parties surveying in remote areas. Stock iron pipe serves both as float well and to support the recorder box. A counterpoise spring replaces the usual weights. As the horizontal recording drum revolves once in 48 hours the chart can be left on for a week since the tidal curve advances in time sufficiently to give a clear record. Tidal ranges from 6 to 25 feet can be accommodated on the chart by fitting appropriate gears.

Inv. no. 1975-38
Source: Lent by the Institute of Oceanographic Sciences

Portable Water Level Recorder, 1964

Portable Water Level Recorder, 1964
Made by R W Munro, London.
No 1861/1028/7
Recorder height: 36 cm, float diameter: 15 cm

A simple recorder for tide or other water surveys. The vertical rotating drum turns at 0.1 inches per hour to give a seven-day curve. Gearing is available to cover a range of 6 to 24 feet. Used by the Admiralty Hydrographic Department in various parts of the world for tidal surveys.

Inv. no. 1975-381   Neg. no. 1123/76
Source: Lent by the Admiralty Hydrographic Department

Pressure Tide Gauge, 1950
Made by Foxboro-Yoxall, Redhill.
No E33211
Recorder height: 55 cm, diaphragm box diameter: 15 cm

This instrument is designed for on-shore reading. The sensing element is a synthetic rubber diaphragm within a metal box. It is connected by tubing to the recording head in which changing pressure is converted to movement of a linkage operating the pen arm. 7-day or 24-hour can be selected for the disc chart.

Inv. no. 1975-382   Neg. no. 1122/76
Sources: Diaphragm given by the maker, Recorder lent by the Admiralty Hydrographic Department

Pressure Tide Gauge, 1950

French Self-Recording Pressure Tide Gauge, 1927
Made by J Richard, Paris
Diameter 22 cm

Designed by L Favé in 1887, this gauge was developed for use in the French Hydrographic Service. Two Bourdon tubes operate a marker pen, scribing onto a smoked glass disk rotated by an eight-day clockwork drive. The gauge could be lowered to 200 metres and could record a tidal range not exceeding 15 metres. The trace was read by means of a special micrometer microscope.

Inv. no. 1927-430 Neg. no. 1121/76
Source: Given by the Service Hydrographique de la Marine, Paris

Recording Tide Gauge, c 1900
Made by Adie
Float Diameter: 23 cm

Vertical recording drum, driven by clockwork, with pen travelling in guides.
This gauge was installed at Chelsea Bridge to collect data for the Chief Engineer's Department, LCC

Inv. no. 1980-559
Source: Given by the Chief Engineer's Department, Greater London Council

Tidal analysis and prediction

Tide-Predicting Machine, Kelvin's First Model, 1872
Made by J. White, Glasgow
Overall height: 24 cm

The model was demonstrated to members of the British Association for the Advancement of Science to show how a mechanical summing of various harmonic motions could speed up the process of tide prediction. Eight pulleys turn on axes at the end of eight cracks of adjustable length, four on the upper and four on the lower side of a wooden frame. A cord, secured at one end, passes round the pulleys and at the other end carries a weight representing the marker. Counterpoise weights are carried in the upper row. The centre of each pulley thus describes a circle of adjustable radius, which circular motion is equivalent to the sum of two simple harmonic motions, one vertical, the other horizontal. Thus the hanging weight describes the required complex motion.

Inv. no. 1881-12 Neg. no. 84
Source: Given by Lord Kelvin

Tide-Predicting Machine, Kelvin's Second Model, 1873
Made by A Légé, London
Overall height: 35 cm

Demonstrates the mechanical addition of two simple harmonic motions. Here, with appropriate gears, the mean lunar and mean solar semi-diurnal constituents are combined. The centres of the two pulleys are given simple harmonic motion in a straight line by means of slides. The integral curve is written on paper on a revolving drum.

Inv. no. 1881-13 Neg. no. 85
Source: Given by the British Association for the Advancement of Science

Tide-Predicting Machine, 1872
Made by A Légé, London
Overall height: 180 cm

This was Kelvin's first working machine. It summed 10 astronomical components to trace the tidal curve for any given place. For each component the machine has a shaft with an overhead crank which carries a pulley pivotted on a parallel axis adjustable for the range applying to that place. The several shafts, their axes parallel, are geared together so that their periods are broadly proportional to the periods of the tidal constituents. On each shaft the crank can be turned and clamped in any position corresponding to the epoch of tide required. The machine was able to draw the tidal curves of one harbour for one year in about four hours.

Inv. no. 1876-1129 Neg. no. 86
Source: Lent by the University of Glasgow

French Self-Recording Pressure Tide Gauge, 1927

Tide-Predicting Machine, Kelvin's First Model, 1872

George Darwin's Tidal Abacus, 1892
Chart size: 60 × 46 cm

Analysis of a tidal curve is made easier by adding up, in vertical columns, the various components that it includes. The abacus has 74 spiked xylonite tablets that can be pinned to a drawing board. Each tablet has compartments for the 24 tidal measurements and is end-stamped with a number specifying the number of the day to which it refers. The tablets are laid on marked paper corresponding to the partial tide chosen. Summing and averaging all 74 numbers standing under the two figure 0s gives the average height of water at 0hrs of that tide, and so forth. Five operations on five different sheets give 370 days' tides. To avoid error the series of sheets is coloured according to the rainbow sequence.

Inv. nos. 1925-947, 1925-948, 1925-949
Neg. no. 1119/76
Source: Lent by the National Physical Laboratory

Tide-Predicting Machine, Kelvin's Second Model, 1873

Miscellaneous

Photograph of the Severn Bore

Taken at The Lower Parting, Gloucester on 4 September 1921.

Inv. no. 1926-539
Source: Purchased

Tide-Predicting Machine, 1872

George Darwin's Tidal Abacus, 1892

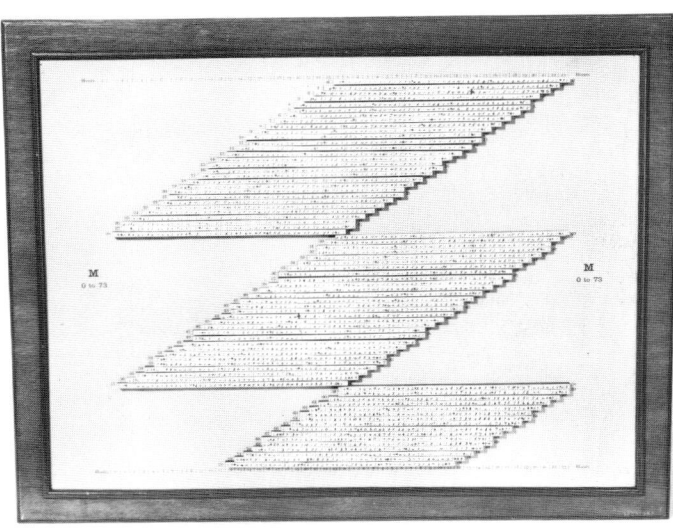

Geomagnetism

The Earth's magnetic field, as we measure it at the surface, is a complex one, arising from eddy currents in the core modified by the ever-changing solar wind which streams past the Earth in its orbit around the sun.

Knowledge of the lodestone and its power to attract iron had probably reached Europe during the 12th century but the behaviour of the compass remained something of a mystery for many centuries thereafter. Men found that the compass needle did not usually point north and south as marked by the sun (geographical north and south), but varied to one side or another. If freely suspended, the needle also tended to dip. As more measurements were made, the degrees of variation and dip were seen to differ from place to place. William Gilbert, author of *De Magnete*, published in 1600, showed that spherical lodestones could serve as models of the Earth in this respect. He moved small pivotted needles over these 'terrellae'. Their alignment corresponded to that of dip needles on the Earth, suggesting that the Earth itself acted as a large magnet.

By the early 18th century accurately pivotted compass needles showed that variation values altered slightly throughout the day, seasonally, and in the long term. Terrestrial magnetism, so important for seafarers, became a regular part of geographical exploration and naval vessels from many nations were instructed to take careful measurements as often as possible so that up-to-date charts were available. Navigators and surveyors have adapted the compass for their own specialized needs. Scientists investigating terrestrial magnetism developed instruments which were particularly sensitive to the *magnetic elements*, that is, variation from geographical north, dip, and magnetic force or intensity. Portable instruments were carried by expeditions on land or sea in order to chart the field with its poles of maximum dip and intensity, and its equator which girdled the Earth in an irregular fashion, swinging north and south of the geographical equator. On land, fixed instruments were set up in observatories to record changes in the magnetic elements with time, both the periodic changes associated with our orbit around the Sun, and the unpredictable storms when pulses of solar energy disrupt the steady behaviour of the needle and often result in the auroral displays seen in the night skies at high latitudes.

Variation compasses

During the late 18th and early 19th centuries the variation or declination compass was commonly a flat pointed needle with its jewel cup turning on a steel pivot, with provision for lifting and clamping the needle when not in use. When the angular distance between geographic and magnetic north was small, as was the case in the majority of northwestern European cities, the needle was confined within a narrow glazed box to shield it from disturbance. Finely-engraved arcs in each end of the box were usually read with the aid of fixed or loose lenses. The needle's tendency to dip was corrected by a sliding counterweight and the box could be set in the geographical meridian with the aid of a supplementary telescope. Where considerable variation was expected, if for example the box was taken on a polar expedition, the compass would have a circular scale.

The small vibration apparatus, invented in 1819 by Christopher Hansteen, Professor of Mathematics at Christiania, and often named after him, measures both variation and horizontal force. Its cylindrical pointed magnet, commonly some 8 to 10 cm long, swings friction-free on a unifilar suspension of silk threads. The complete apparatus consists of a square glazed box on three footscrews, with a glass or brass cylinder topped by the suspension pulley. The silk threads pass down the cylinder and the magnet hangs from a small stirrup, revolving over a circular scale on the floor of the box. A rod passes into the box, allowing the operator to steady the needle between observations. Intensity is measured by vibrating the needle and timing its rate of swing past a datum mark, this rate being controlled by the strength of the local force. The vibration apparatus may include a thermometer (to correct the intensity measurements) and a box of spare and dummy magnets, the latter being used to untwist and stretch the silk threads.

Variation Compass by Adams, c 1750

Late 18th century
Engraved: Royal Society 39
Believed to have been used for observing the effects of the aurora upon the magnetic needle.

12 inch edge-bar needle, 1 × 2mm, on square rock-crystal bearing, with two brass sliding counterpoises. The fittings for raising the needle off its pivot now missing. In glazed brass box, with brass arcs 20°E–W divided to 1°.

Inv. no. 1900-130   Neg. no. 183/52
Source: Lent by the Royal Society

By Adams, c 1750
Signed: Gowin Knight Invt. Made by George Adams Instrut Maker to the Prince of Wales in fleet street London.

10 inch bar magnet with chalcedony cup on a steel pivot. Brass counterbalance slide.

Cavendish's Variation Compass, late 18th century

Brass scale, 10° E–W, divided to ½°, read by microscope. Glazed brass box.

Inv. no. 1910-127   Neg. no. 959
Source: Purchased

Cavendish's, late 18th century
See also: 1930-903, Cavendish's dip circle, page 30.

12 inch bar magnet on unifilar suspension. Brass counterbalance slide. Scales 28° E–W, divided to 10′, read by independent microscopes. Glazed wooden box. With dummy bar and sighting telescope. Unsigned. Formerly belonged to Henry Cavendish who was occupied with magnetic observations from 1759 to 1809.

Inv. no. 1930-902   Neg. no. 7062
Source: Given by the Duke of Devonshire

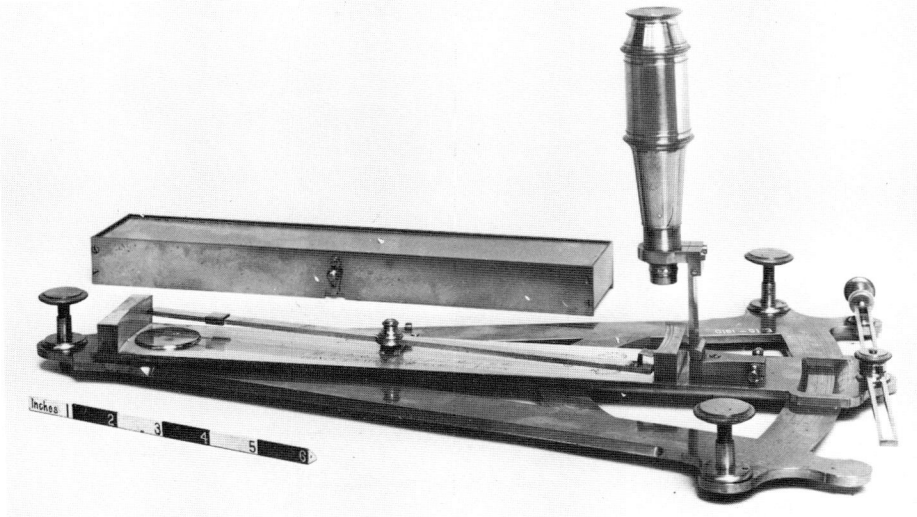

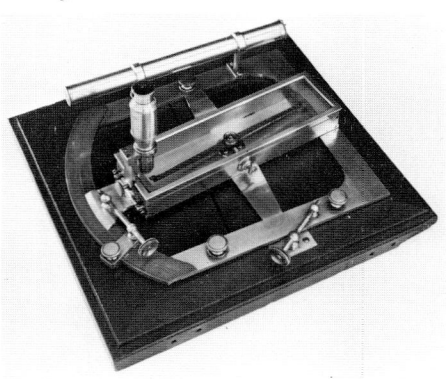

Variation Compass by T Blunt, early 19th century

By T Blunt, early 19th century
*Signed: T Blunt. No 22. Cornhill London.
[Thomas Blunt fl 1760–1822 but his successor
Thomas Harris appears to have traded as
'Blunt' from 1822–1827, working from 22
Cornhill until 1814 and between 1820–27.]*

Flat 7½ inch magnet, on agate bearing,
fitted at each end with brass terminals
engraved with index line. These lie
horizontal to ungraduated silvered arcs in
the magnet box. Brass frame scale 47° E–W
divided to ½° with vernier read by
microscope. Glazed magnet box on brass
frame which is capable of fine sideways
adjustment by screw, after which it may be
clamped to the wooden base. A 10 inch
telescope alongside serves to find the
geographical meridian.

Inv. no. 1917-109   Neg. no. 62/79
Source: Given by T H Court

Unsigned, probably early 19th century

13 inch vertical strip magnet, agate cup,
sliding counterweight. Silver arcs 25° E–W
divided to ½°. Silver longitudinal base plate
with index line and provision for a fitting
(unknown, now missing). In a glazed
wooden box.

Inv. no. 1979-243
Source: Transferred from the Wellcome
Museum of the History of Medicine

Unsigned, probably early 19th century

2½ inch magnet, unifilar suspension. Ivory
scale, two 70° arcs divided to 1° to 50° each
way, then to 5°. Wooden suspension tube.
Incomplete.

Inv. no. 1980-1886
Source: Given by the Meteorological Office

By Robinson, fl 1821–34
Signed: Robinson London

3⅜ inch magnet, unifilar suspension.
Circular paper scale divided to 1°. Brass
suspension tube. With brass dummy needle
and spare magnet.

Inv. no. 1914-146
Source: Given by the Meteorological Office

By Robinson, fl 1821–34
*Signed: Robinson 38 Devonshire St Portland
Place London*

[4 inch needle missing] Paper scale divided
to 1°. Brass suspension tube.

Inv. no. 1980-1885
Source: Given by the Meteorological Office

Unsigned, early 19th century
Box engraved: I.40

2⅝ inch magnet, unifilar suspension. Ivory
scale, divided to 1°. Brass suspension tube.
   Accessories: Needle box with two
magnets

Inv. no. 1876-798   Neg. no. 61/79
Source: Given by Kew Observatory

Variation Compass, early 19th century

By Barrow & Co, fl 1848–64
*Signed: Henry Barrow & Comp 26 Oxendon
St London*
Used by Sir John Richardson and William
   Pullen on the Arctic expeditions searching
   for Sir John Franklin

Two 6 inch strip magnets, counterbalance
cross, and circular scale form an assembly
which can hang on a unifilar suspension or
rest on a pivot turning in a ruby cup. Silver
scale divided to 6′, read by two microscopes.
Two spirit levels. Glazed brass box.

Inv. no. 1876-790   Neg. nos. 57/79, 60/79
Source: Given by the Meteorological Office

Variation Compass by Barrow & Co, fl 1848–64

**'Admiralty pattern' unsigned, late 19th
century**

Admiralty pattern dry compass card with 4
composite magnets, 7¼ and 4¾ inch, 2
sliding counterweights. Scale divided to ½°.
Shades, sight vane, mirror, spirit level on
rotating frame.

Inv. no. 1980-1878
Source: Given by the Meteorological Office

Unifilar Magnetometer by Brunner, 1884
Signed: Brunner fres à Paris

Small but sturdy precision instrument made
as a companion to dip circle 1889–62, as
used during the Magnetic Survey of France,
1884–86. Collimator magnet 6.5 cm
   Circles divided to ½°, with verniers;
vertical circle has rotating microscopes.
   Like the Kew unifilars, it can be set up to
measure variation, or, rearranged, to
measure horizontal force.
   Accessories: spare magnet, dummy, tools
etc in fitted carrying box.

Inv. no. 1889-63   Neg. no. 63/79
Source: Purchased from the maker

Deviation Test Compass
French, prob. late 19th century. Unsigned

Pointed 19 cm needle, brass cup.
Hand-inked card, 4 scales, divided to 2°.
Scales marked:
(E–N–W) Series pour les deviations à droite.
(N–W–S) Series pour les vaccourcissements.
(N–E–S) Series pour les prolongements.
(E–S–W) Series pour les deviations à
gauche.
Asterisk at 24°W prob. marks magnetic N.
Fitted in square box.

Inv. no. 1980-1877   Neg. no. 455/84
Source: Transferred from the Wellcome
Museum of the History of Medicine

Deviation Test Compass

Walker's Portable Variometer, 1913
Made by Cambridge Scientific Instrument Company Ltd, No 19451
Overall height: 27 cm

Designed by George Walker to provide absolute horizontal force values at each station during the magnetic resurvey of the British Isles, 1913–15. The variometer fitted directly into the Elliott unifilar (No 66) used on the survey. It consists of a cylindrical magnet 2cm by 1mm diameter, on a quartz fibre suspension, with torsion head and clamp all housed within an insulated brass tube. A mirror is fixed vertically along the fibre, its plane at right angles to the magnet. A telescope projects opposite the mirror, supported on a rigid frame. Light enters through a prism on the telescope tube, is reflected by the mirror, and casts the image of a vertical fibre on to a horizontal 100-division scale in the telescope's focal plane. Estimating the probable range, Walker hoped to detect differences of 2 or 3 gamma, applying corrections for temperature and other factors, but was less successful than he had anticipated.

Inv. no. 1930-196
Source: Lent by the Royal Society

Variation Needle, early 19th century

12 inch bar magnet fitted with sliding brass counterpoises and an agate cap.

Inv. no. 1900-130
Source: Lent by the Royal Society

Dip circles

A magnetic needle on a horizontal axis lays horizontally only at the magnetic equator; elsewhere its dip or inclination increases, approaching the vertical at the poles of maximum dip.

The dip circle consists of a pointed needle, commonly between 15 and 25 cm long, pierced by a steel axis which rolls on flat agate planes or, if the instrument is intended for use at sea, is carried in agate cups. It is enclosed in a glazed box, either circular and made of brass, or wooden, and square in form, the latter being easier to handle in sub-zero polar temperatures. There is provision for lifting and clamping the needle. The circular scale, originally inside the box, was later usually set outside, with verniers, and two microscopes on a revolving plate, so that very precise readings could be made. The glazed box revolves over a lower graduated circle and stands on three footscrews. One or two spirit levels may be attached to the frame. In use, the box is aligned with the magnetic meridian to minimise friction from horizontal magnetic forces. A box of spare needles is often provided, the full sequence of operations requiring that the apparatus, and one or more needles, be reversed to repeat the measurements, the accepted dip value being the average of many observations.

Dip Circle by Nairne & Blunt, c 1775

By Nairne and Blunt, c 1775
Signed: Made by Nairne & Blunt Cornhill London. Royal Society No 38

12 inch blunt-pointed needle with index line and crosstree.

Silver scale divided to 20'. Small arcs divided to 1° are fitted opposite the 70° to 75° sectors to avoid errors of parallax when reading the scale. (This instrument was made when the dip angle in London was about 72°).

Brass box, two spirit levels on top. Brass plate engraved with radial lines at 15° intervals and carying a perpendicular index.

Inv. no. 1900-129   Neg. nos. 64/79, 118/68
Source: Lent by the Royal Society

Dip Circle by Dollond, c 1820

Cavendish's late, 18th century
Unsigned.
Formerly the property of Henry Cavendish
See also: 1930-902, Cavendish's variation compass, page 27.

Pointed 8¾ needle, axis carried in the ends of two adjustable brass screws and can be clamped for transport. Silver circle divided to 30', suspended from a rotatable brass disc divided to 1°. To align the instrument, a wooden arm with a small gimballed compass at one end, is clamped to this disc.

Inv. no. 1930-903
Source: Given by the Duke of Devonshire

By Robinson, c 1830
Signed: Robinson 38 Devonshire St Portland Place London
Supplied to HMS Terror for the Colonial Magnetic Observatories expedition, 1839–43

Six-inch pointed needle, on agate planes. Brass circle divided to 20'. Blackened brass box, spirit level on top (missing), revolving lenses. Brass plate divided to 1°.
With pair of 6" bar magnets and wooden holder for magnetising needle.

Inv. no. 1876-804
Source: Given by the Admiralty Hydrographic Department

By Dollond, c 1820
Signed: Dollond London and (on box) I.11

Two 11½ inch rounded needles, index engraved at tips, on agate planes. Silver scale divided to 20'. Brass box, two spirit levels on top. Base plate engraved with lines at 45°. Needle box with brass dummy, dip, variation and intensity needles, all with keepers; counterweighted pivot.

Inv. no. 1876-805   Neg. no. 992
Source: Given by the Admiralty Hydrographic Department

By Nairne and Blunt, early 19th century
Signed: Nairne & Blunt London I.9

Nine inch pointed needle, in agate cups. Silver scale divided to 20'.
As this instrument was intended for use at sea when the ship's motion prevented the needle from coming to rest, there are sliding pointers on the circle that can be moved to its mean position.
Brass box, suspended thermometer inside, graduated from −38°F to 148°F (engraved: Thos Jones & Sons 62 Charing Cross). Hangs in gimbals from a wooden stand.
Azimuth plate (4 inch diam.) above frame with sighting vane, divided to 1°.
Wooden arm with a small gimballed compass at its far end can be clamped to the upper plate and the whole apparatus thus aligned with the magnetic meridian.

Inv. no. 1876-806
Source: Given by the Admiralty Hydrographic Department

By Robinson, fl 1821 to 1834
Signed: Robinson London

9½ inch pointed needle, on quartz planes. Brass scale divided to 20'.
Wooden box, spirit level inside, revolving lenses.
Base plate divided to ½°.

Inv. no. 1980-1882
Source: Given by the Meteorological Office

By Robinson, fl 1821–34
Signed: Robinson 38 Devonshire St Portland Place London

Four pointed 6 inch needles; one with subaxial weight, one pierced with three holes towards end tip. On agate planes.
Brass scale divided to 20'.
Brass box, spirit level on top, rotating lenses. Thermometer (0°–140°F) behind circle.
Base plate divided to 1°.
With fitted wooden case holding two needle boxes, counterweight and variation needle, two supplementary lenses, spirit level.

Inv. no. 1900-79
Source: Given by Miss Radford

By Robinson, c 1834
Signed: Robinson 38 Devonshire St, Portland Place, London
Used by Sir James Clark Ross between 1839 and 1843 on the Colonial Magnetic Observatories expedition

Two six-inch pointed needles, on agate planes.
Silver scale divided to 20'.
Brass box, spirit level on top, revolving lenses.
Base plate divided to 1°.
Needle box.

Inv. no. 1876-789
Source: Lent by the Kew Committee of the Royal Society

By Robinson, fl 1821–34

As 1876-789 (But has no needle)

Inv. no. 1980-1881
Source: Given by the Meteorological Office

By Robinson and Barrow, fl 1845–47
Signed: Robinson & Barrow. Successors to the late Mr T C Robinson, 38 Devonshire Strt, Portland Place London

9½ inch pointed needle, on quartz planes. Silver scale divided to 10'.
Wooden box, spirit level inside on base, rotating lenses.
Base plate divided to 1°
Needle box with variation needle and counterweighted pivot.

Inv. no. 1915-145
Source: Given by the Meteorological Office

Fox Dip Circle by George, mid 19th century
Signed: W George. Falmouth. C.10

Two 7 inch pointed needles with ⅞ inch brass pulleys on the axis, in agate cups.
Silver scale divided to 15'.
Blackened brass box, revolving lenses. Two spirit levels below. Thermometer inside box on back plate, graduated 10°F to 240°F and centigrade equivalents. (Engraved: George. Falmouth).
Accessories for intensity measurements: two deflector-magnet holders; hooks, weights and forceps for hanging weights on needle pulley; ivory rubber to vibrate the needle axis.
Intended for use on a moving ship, this is a heavy apparatus, with needles held in cup bearings, able to measure dip and intensity. Similar instruments were taken by James Clark Ross on the Colonial Magnetic Observatories expedition, 1939–43.

Inv. no. 1908-97   Neg. nos. 113/69, 114/69
Source: Given by the Admiralty

Fox Dip Circle by George, mid 19th century

By Barrow, c 1846
Signed: Barrow Successor to T C Robinson London

Two 9½ inch pointed needles, on quartz planes.
Brass scale divided to 20'.
Wooden box, spirit level inside.
Revolving lenses.
Base plate divided to ½°, with vernier.
Needle box.

Inv. no. 1980-1883
Source: Given by the Meteorological Office

By Barrow, fl 1848–64
Signed: Henry Barrow & Co 26 Oxendon St London

Two 3½ inch pointed needles, on agate planes.
Silver scale divided to ½° with verniers and revolving lenses.
Wooden box, spirit level inside.
Base plate divided to ½°.
With Lloyd-Creak attachment to clamp a second needle outside the box for intensity measurements.
Wooden holder for magnetising needle.
Needle box.

Inv. no. 1980-1879   Neg. no. 457/84
Source: Given by the Meteorological Office

Dip Circle by Barrow, fl 1848–64

By Barrow, fl 1848–64

As 1980–1879 (But does not have Lloyd-Creak attachment).

Inv. no. 1980-1880
Source: Given by the Meteorological Office

By Brunner, 1889
Signed: Brunner Frères
Similar to that used by Moureaux during the Magnetic Survey of France, 1884–86

Two 6.5 cm pointed needles, on agate planes.
Silver scale divided to 30'.
Brass box, revolving mirrors, verniers, microscopes.
Base plate divided to 30', with vernier (read with hand lens).
Fitted box with lens, tools, plumbline.

Inv. no. 1889-62   Neg. no. 55/79
Source: Purchased from the maker

By Dover, 1889
Signed: Dover Charlton Kent Circle 94.
Used by Thorpe in 1891 and by Rücker in 1892 during the Magnetic Survey of Gt Britain

Identical to 1930-195.
With needle box and boxed pair of 9 inch bar magnets.

Inv. no. 1889-23   Neg. no. 137/79
Source: Purchased from the maker

By Dover, c 1890
Signed: Dover Charlton Kent Circle 99
Made for the Magnetic Survey of the British Isles 1890–2, and used in the resurvey, 1913–15.

Two 3½ inch pointed needles, on agate planes.
Silver scale divided to ½°.
Wooden box, spirit level below, outside box. Revolving microscopes are aligned on the needle tips, the scale is then read with vernier and revolving lenses.
Base plate divided to ½°, with vernier.
In fitted wooden box with accessories.

Inv. no. 1930-195   Neg. nos. 727/79, 728/79
Source: Lent by the Royal Society

Dip Needles

Two dip needles used by Sir James Ross. Flat pointed 6 inch needles, weighted at one centre edge. In fitted box.
Inv. no. 1915-151
Source: Given by the Meteorological Office

Two Fox dip circle magnets in carriers, with ivory rubber.
Inv. no. 1980-1884
Source: Given by the Meteorological Office

Flat pointed 7 inch dip needle in metal box.
Inv. no. 1980-1894
Source: Given by the Meteorological Office

Demonstration model, 10 cm dip needle on stand, made by BTL.
Inv. no. 1981-127
Source: Transferred from the Wellcome Museum of the History of Medicine

Dip Circle by Dover, c 1890

Kew pattern unifilar magnetometers

A larger and more elaborate version of Hansteen's vibration apparatus, this magnetometer, made to a standard approved by Kew Observatory, served both as portable and observatory apparatus, able to measure both variation and horizontal intensity. It consists essentially of a lower divided circle, supported on three footscrews, and an upper concentric circle, carried on a common axis. The upper circle has two verniers and reading microscopes. The variation magnet, which hangs on a unifilar silk suspension within a wooden chamber, is a steel tube commonly 8 to 10 cm long, with a lens at one end focussed on a fine transport scale at the other. It acts as a collimator and an image of the scale is viewed through a co-axial telescope focussed for infinity. A thermometer is also set into the magnet chamber.

When set up to measure horizontal intensity a brass inertia bar is added to the stirrup, to find the magnet's moment of inertia. The collimator magnet is then set in a carriage at various distances along a graduated bar, and its deflection of the central magnet used to compute the local horizontal intensity. Tool-kits of screwdrivers and tommy-bars, spare lenses, reels of silk and spare magnets may be found in the fitted instrument-boxes of these magnetometers.

By Thomas Jones, KO No 106.
See also: 1915-148, inertia bar, page 35.
Signed: Thomas Jones 4 Rupert Street London
Inv. no. 1915-144   Neg. no. 56/79
Source: Given by the Meteorological Office.

By Thomas Jones, KO No 102.
Base and deflector parts missing.
Inv. no. 1980-1887
Source: Given by the Meteorological Office.

By Thomas Jones, KO No 5.
(Suspension missing)
Inv. no. 1980-1890
Source: Given by the Meteorological Office.

KO No 6.
(No maker's name; magnet missing)
Inv. no. 1980-1891
Source: Given by the Meteorological Office.

By Elliott Bros, London.
No 57, in fitted box. Incomplete. Magnets: 2.5 cm
Inv. no. 1983-332
Source: Given by University College, London.

Kew Pattern Unifilar Magnetometer by Thomas Jones

Observatory magnetometers

These are intended to register large or small fluctuations in the magnetic field at any one place and also to detect the slow secular, long-term changes in global magnetism. Three instruments are normally installed, measuring variation, horizontal and vertical force. Data are analysed to give values for variation, dip, horizontal and vertical intensities, relative to the absolute values which can also be measured from time to time. Only a continuous register will reveal the smallest and most rapid movements. Observations were made at frequent intervals in the Colonial Magnetic Observatories but by 1845 photography had become a possible means of securing a permanent continuous record. First used at Greenwich Observatory, it was soon in use at Kew where the Superintendent, Sir Francis Ronalds, experimented with various photographic magnetometers during the later 1840s, followed there by John Walsh during the 1850s.

Large magnetometers, housed in iron-free buildings, had to be well-spaced to avoid mutual interference of their magnets. Mascart's suite of instruments was to be installed in the equable temperature of a deep cellar and had therefore to be much smaller, as two sets were operated, one to be read directly and the other providing a photographic record.

Colonial Magnetic Observatories Magnetometers, 1839
Made by Grubb of Dublin.
This set of magnetometers was originally installed at St Helena Observatory.

A suite of three instruments:
1. Declinometer. 15 inch bar magnet with collimator arrangements of lens and scale, hanging on fibres of untwisted silk, the magnet assembly enclosed in a circular wooden box with viewing panels.
2. Horizontal force magnetometer. 15 inch bar magnet on wire bifilar suspension, hanging at right angles to the meridian. In wooden box, as 1.
3. Vertical force magnetometer. A light 12 inch magnet carrying a brass frame with crosswires at each end. Set up as a balance, but the bearings and viewing microscopes are now missing.

Inv. no. 1876-796   Neg. nos. 517/81, 518/81
Source: Lent by the Royal Society

Colonial Magnetic Observatories Magnetometers, 1839

Brooke's Photographic Magnetometers, 1846 and later
Unsigned

Parts of the unifilar declinometer and bifilar horizontal force magnetometers, with gas jets and photographic recording drums, as designed by Charles Brooke for Greenwich Observatory in 1846 and subsequently modified for display at the 1851 Exhibition and for later use.

Inv. no. 1876-841 to 1876-846
Source: Lent by the inventor

Ronalds' Photographic Horizontal Force Magnetometer, 1847

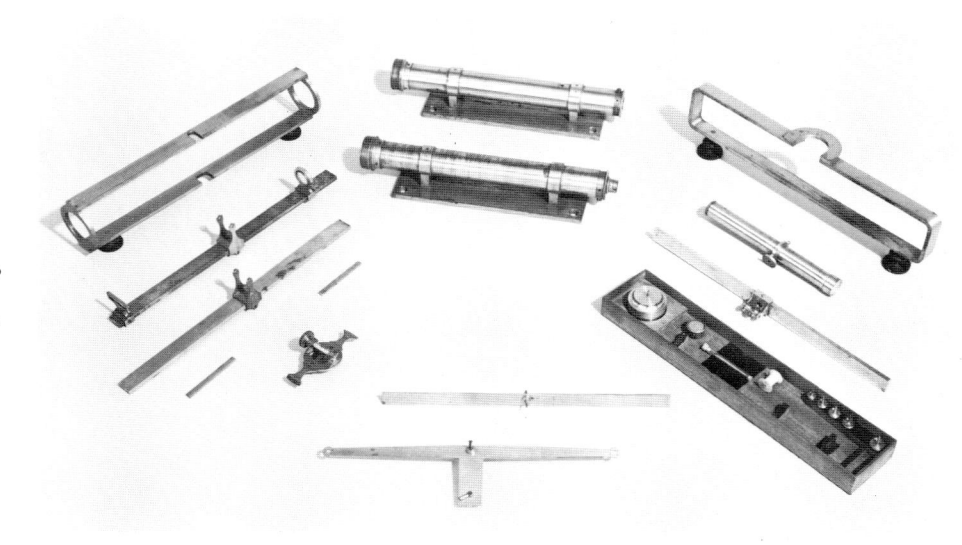

Ronalds' Photographic Horizontal Force Magnetometer, 1847
Unsigned

Bifilar wire suspension (not original) carries the 15 inch bar magnet, under which is a brass bar and shutter. Light from an oil lamp passes through a hole in this shutter and is focussed by a lens onto a silvered daguerreotype plate drawn steadily upwards by clockwork.

Francis Ronalds constructed this magnetometer at Kew Observatory where it provided continuous records of horizontal force. The traces on the plates were sometimes etched in and engravings taken, or tracings were made, in which case the silvered plates could be reused.

Inv. no. 1876-786   Neg. no. 488/84
Source: Given by the Meteorological Office.

Ronalds' Photographic Vertical Force Magnetograph, 1847
Unsigned

Installed at Kew Observatory and modified in later years. Now incomplete.

Inv. no. 1876-788
Source: Given by Kew Observatory

Mascart's Observatory Magnetometers, 1883
Signed: Ateliers Ruhmkorff J Charpentier Ingr Constr Paris

Suite of three magnetometers small enough to install together without each magnet disturbing the others.
1   Declinometer. 5 cm square bar magnet, on unifilar silk suspension, carries a suspended mirror. Below stands a fixed mirror, the whole enclosed in a brass box with a 1 metre lens as viewing panel. A graduated ivory scale faces the mirrors and a distant telescope, reading its reflected image, observes the magnet's declination. Numbered 577-3.
2   Horizontal force magnetometer. As 1, but with the magnet on wire bifilar suspension. Numbered 524-3.
3   Vertical force magnetometer. Flat vertical magnet balanced on agate planes with horizontal attached and reference mirrors sighted via a prism on top of the balance box. Fitted thermometer. Numbered 575-3.
4   Deflector carrier and scale. For calibrating the bifilar and balance magnetometers.
    Made by J. Charpentier of Paris to Mascart's design, two sets of magnetometers could be installed in a cellar free of temperature variation, to be read directly and photographically.
5   Control clock with lamp; prisms for receiving the reflected rays and passing them to the photographic plate.

Inv. nos. 1884-58 to 1884-62
Neg. nos. 458/84 to 462/84
Source: Purchased from the maker

Mascart's Observatory Magnetometers, 1883

Dip Inductor by Schulze, 1913
Signed: G Schulze Werkst. f. Precisions-Mechanik Potsdam No 103
Installed at Eskdalemuir Observatory in 1913 and used there for absolute measurements of dip and intensity until 1958.

Invented by H Wild as an alternative to the dip circle for absolute dip and intensity measurements. The inductor consists of a coil of insulated wire which can be rotated about an axis, itself rotatable about two other perpendicular axes. The coil windings are connected by a commutator and a galvanometer. Current induced in the coil by the earth's field can be detected or measured, depending on the manner in which the inductor is used.

Inv. no. 1976-649   Neg. no. 453/84
Source: Lent by the Institute of Geological Sciences

Dip Inductor by Schulze, 1913

Inertia Rings and Bars

Bar, 4 inches, in case.
See also: 1915-144, Unifilar magnetometer, above.
Inv. no. 1915-148
Source: Given by the Meteorological Office

Boxed ring, 3⁹⁄₁₆ inches diameter.
Inked on box 'From vibration box Kew Feb 12 '57 Cap^n Collinson'.
Inv. no. 1915-149
Source: Given by the Meteorological Office

Assorted rings of various thicknesses.
2 of 3⅝ inches diameter, 7 of 3 inches, 1 of 2¹³⁄₁₆ inches; 6 discs of 2 inches to 1⅞ inches. One ring inked 'Capt Kellett's ring'. One inked 'Enterprise'.
Inv. no. 1980-1869
Source: Given by the Meteorological Office

Boxed set of 6 bars, 3¾ to 4 inches.
Inv. no. 1980-1870
Source: Given by the Meteorological Office

Boxed pair of rings.
Ms label in lid gives dimensions as 'copper: 3.486″ diam. brass: 2.324″ diam. Oct 7 1853'.
Inv. no. 1980-1871   Neg. no. 456/84
Source: Given by the Meteorological Office

Boxed set of three bars, 4 inches.
Inv. no. 1980-1872   Neg. no. 454/84
Source: Given by the Meteorological Office

Boxed copper ring, 3⁷⁄₁₆ inches diameter.
Punched 'M.N.O.P.'
Inv. no. 1980-1873
Source: Given by the Meteorological Office

Boxed pair of brass rings, 3⅝ inches diameter.
Box inked on base 'Enterprise Cap^n Collinson'.
Inv. no. 1980-1874
Source: Given by the Meteorological Office

Collection of 11 bars, 3½ to 4 inches; various collimator tubes and cases.
Inv. no. 1980-1876
Source: Given by the Meteorological Office

Boxed Inertia Bars

Boxed Inertia Rings

Terrellae and Magnetic Models

Terrellae

Terrella.
4½ inch diameter, on wooden base.
Inv. no. 1931-679   Neg. no. 4853
Source: Lent by the Royal Society

Terrella.
3 inch diameter, in iron clamp with small steel roller in front, on wooden base.
Inv. no. 1931-680   Neg. no. 4853
Source: Lent by the Royal Society

Globe demonstrating the phenomena of terrestrial magnetism.
Insulated copper wire is wound round the 'equator' of a hollow iron globe. Current is sent through the wire, and the globe turned on its axis, to move small magnetic needles on the axis frame, thus showing declination patterns on the globe surface.
Inv. no. 1872-50
Source: Purchased from the maker, Elliott Bros

Globe demonstrating the phenomena of terrestrial magnetism.
An elaborate model consisting of two geographical globes, one rotating within the other, on separate axles. Both globes are wound with insulated wire and the ocean one is covered with thin sheet-iron to produce a different magnetic effect. Current is passed through the wires and the internal globe rotated, to show secular and geographical variation across the world.
Inv. no. 1894-18
Source: Given by the inventor, Henry Wilde FRS

Model of magnetic surface.
Plaster representation of the annual and diurnal variation of declination based on Dr Bache's measurements at Philadelphia, 1840–45.
Inv. no. 1900-128
Source: Lent by the Royal Society

Model of magnetic surface.
Similar to 1900-128
30 × 36 × 16 cm.
Inv. no. 1980-1895
Source: Given by the Meteorological Office

Globe showing magnetic elements in 1872

Globe.
Marked with the four magnetic elements for the year 1872: contours of absolute intensity, four points of maximum intensity, two dip poles and the magnetic equator.
Inv. no. 1876-812   Neg. no. 58/79
Source: Lent by the Admiralty Hydrographic Dept

Two world charts.
Marked with contours of equal dip and variation for the year 1880.
Inv. nos. 1921-1056 and 1057
Source: [Found]

Miscellaneous

Boxed Pairs of Magnets

Bars 12⅛″ × 1¼″ × ¼″, with keepers, undated
Inv. no. 1981-129
Source: Transferred from the Wellcome Museum of the History of Medicine

Bars 6⅛″ × ¾″ × ¼″, with keepers, undated
Inv. no. 1981-128
Source: Transferred from the Wellcome Museum of the History of Medicine

Cabinet of magnetic apparatus.
By W & S Jones, early 19th century. Contains magnetic and non-magnetic shapes and models for demonstrating general and terrestrial magnetism.
Inv. no. 1936-441
Source: Given by Mrs M J Mackay

Thomson's Magnetic Balance
Engraved: Sir William Thomson's Vertical Force Instrument No 21 J. White, Glasgow

3 inch rod magnet, transverse knife axis in cups, paper counterweight. Vertical paper scales. 0–3 cm divided in mm. Horizontal counterweight scale. Black brass cylindrical box with end-glasses. Bubble level and suspension rings.

Inv. no. 1946-216
Source: Given by the National Physical Laboratory

Research in the Ionosphere

Automatic Ionospheric Height Recorder, 1949
Made by Union Radio Co Ltd to specifications issued by the National Physical Laboratory Serial 6 Mk II.

The ionosphere is in a state of constant and complex motion, partly random, due to the fluctuating solar wind interacting with the earth's magnetic field. Ionospheric properties are regularly investigated at a worldwide network of stations by an automatic radio-echo technique in which short bursts of radio waves of different frequencies are emitted at vertical incidence and the resulting reflected waves registered as an 'ionogram'. The recorder consists of five units:
i) A crystal-controlled frequency divider unit.
ii) A linear time-base generator.
iii) A pulse-modulated transmitter.
iv) A receiver, tuned to the transmitter through a servo-system.
v) A display unit: two cathode ray tubes, one of which is recorded photographically.
In mobile cabinet 93 × 85 × 130 cm high.

Inv. no. 1981-825
Source: Presented by the British Antarctic Survey

Rocket Payload Components used in Aurora Investigations, c 1973

Two geiger counters and power pack. Cylindrical analyser, sectioned. 6-stage Cockcroft-Walton voltage multiplier. 24-stage Cockcroft-Walton voltage multiplier assembly. 12 v – 2000 v DC/DC/converter. Servo control unit. Particle detector, amplifier and pulse height discriminator.

Inv. nos. 1977-148 to 1977-150
Source: Lent by Science Research Council

Geophysical prospecting

The geophysical prospector uses various physical principles to 'see' underground by detecting characteristic differences between adjacent rock bodies. Such differences may be explained in terms of subsurface structure, and give an indication where test drilling might be undertaken for minerals, oil or gas. The main properties exhibited by the more common rocks are: density, magnetism, elasticity and electrical conductivity, while occasionally radioactivity and temperature anomalies may be measured. The survey methods and their principal applications are:

Seismic reflection and refraction	– Exploration for oil and gas. Regional geological surveys. Site surveys for engineering projects.
Gravity	– Exploration for oil and gas. Regional and detailed geological studies.
Magnetic	– Exploration for oil and gas and certain minerals. Regional and detailed geological studies. Archaeological surveys.
Electrical and electromagnetic	– Exploration for certain minerals. Local site surveys. Archaeological surveys.
Radiometric	– Exploration for radioactive minerals.

In prospecting by gravity, magnetic, radiometric and self-potential electrical methods, local naturally-occurring variations within the earth are measured. Seismic and most electrical methods involve an input of artificial energy (an explosion or an electric current), and measurement of the consequent reaction of subsurface rock bodies.

Geophysical methods were used in mineral prospecting from the 17th century when the magnetic compass was employed to search for buried iron ore deposits. However specialised instruments were not developed until the latter part of the 19th century. From 1915–20 dip needles of various types were introduced for magnetic prospecting and air-borne magnetometers which were used for submarine detection during World War 2 were employed for geophysical prospecting soon afterwards. Nuclear magnetometers for ground and air-borne surveys appeared around 1955 and the optical pumping type magnetomers around 1961.

Electrical prospecting, first considered theoretically by Robert Fox in 1815, became a practical proposition during the 1920s with a variety of electrode configurations being used.

The earliest application of geophysical methods to oil exploration involved searching for likely geological formations within which oil might be trapped. In 1898 Eötvös developed a torsion balance for exploration capable of measuring the distortions in the earth's gravitational field caused by salt domes where oil might be located. Various modifications of this balance, many employing photographic registration, were introduced in the early part of the 20th century. Seismic refraction equipment was used to search for possible oil-bearing formations after Mintrop developed his field seismograph in 1919. Mintrop seismographs and various torsion balances were used to discover many oilfields in North America, and, after 1928, in Iran. Karcher carried out experiments using seismic reflection methods during 1919–21. To replace the cumbersome torsion balance simple pendulum systems were introduced around 1932 and in 1935 the first gravimeter giving direct readings of gravity differences came into use. Since World War 2 lightweight gravity meters have made rapid surveys possible; such instruments can be placed on the sea bed or used on board ship.

Exploration Seismographs

Field seismographs rely on explosive charges, accurately timed, sending energy waves through subsurface layers to the receiving apparatus. Refraction seismology interprets the waves which are refracted and delayed by passage through different strata. Reflection seismology detects waves reflected at a subsurface profile to geophones laid across the exploration zone and thence to a recorder. To keep the explosive charges small, a high degree of sensitivity is required whilst at the same time the equipment has to be easy to transport and use in rough terrain.

Mintrop Seismograph, c 1921
Made by Seismos GmbH Hannover
Height of Seismometer unit overall: 72 cms

Designed by Lutger Mintrop, this is the earliest practical field seismograph. It detects the vertical component of ground motion through a lead sphere carried on a leaf spring. The motion is initially magnified by lever action of the aluminium cone. The cone vertex rotates a spindle with attached mirror. A light-beam from the recorder box is reflected from the mirror and again magnified before the beam is recorded photographically on a moving chart together with a time-trace. The explosive charge was set off at a known distance and reached the instrument as an air-borne pressure wave giving the exact time of the start of each operation.

Inv. no. 1931-766   Neg. nos. 854/57, 855/57
Source: Lent by the Geophysical Co Ltd

Microid Seismograph, 1928
Made by Griffin & Tatlock Ltd
Overall Height 68 cms

In this instrument, designed by J H Jones, the motion of the lead mass is magnified magnetically. The aluminium cone carries a phosphor-bronze strip with attached soft iron element and mirror. The iron is placed in the field between two magnets and therefore rotates as the cone moves. The movement is recorded photographically by reflecting a light beam from the mirror. In this way a total magnification of 50,000 is obtained.

Inv. no. 1976-35 Neg. nos. 4850, 4851, 4852
Source: Given by Mr L M Parr

Portable Refraction Seismograph, c 1960
Made by Geospace, model GT 2A
Overall length 46 cm

Signals from up to 12 geophones are received, converted to light beams and recorded by a Polaroid camera.

Inv. no. 1980-679
Source: Given by Wimpey Laboratories Ltd

Creating and detecting seismic waves

Geophones (and hydrophones) detect seismic waves created by explosions or other forms of high-energy pulse. In a geophone the seismic waves are converted into oscillating electrical signals by a moving-coil and magnet system or a pressure-sensitive piezo-electric crystal detector. On land the geophones are set firmly into the ground; at sea hydrophones can be lowered to the sea bed or towed in a buoyant cable.

Geophone, c 1955 (sectioned)

Suspended coil, moving against a fixed magnet.

Inv. no. 1955-1
Source: Lent by W G Pye & Co Ltd

Air Gun, c 1969

Generates a seismic pulse by emitting a blast of highly-compressed air.

Inv. no. 1978-422
Source: Lent by Geophysical Service International

Pop-up Bottom Seismic Recorder, 1969
(Scale model 1:24)

Hydrophone and recorder are carried on a frame to which a buoy and sinker are attached. When the seismic survey is done acoustic signals from a parent ship trigger the sinker release gear and the buoy lifts the recorder back to the surface for recovery.

Inv. no. 1977-42
Source: Made in the Science Museum

Section of a Marine Hydrophone Streamer, 1969 (partly sectioned)

Piezo-electric hydrophones and their cables are arranged along a buoyant polythene tube, towed through the sea.

Inv. no. 1978-423
Source: Lent by Geophysical Service International

Section of a Marine Hydrophone Streamer, 1984

Made-up sample of 24-channel high resolution seismic streamer.

Inv. no. 1984-674
Source: Given by Geophysical Systems Ltd.

Exploration gravity meters

A very small mass, counter-balanced against the general pull of the earth's gravity, will still respond to small local variations caused by rocks of different densities. Great care has to be taken to protect such delicate systems from temperature change and other outside effects, but if this can be done extremely compact, lightweight, field apparatus can be constructed.

The Cavendish type torsion balance was adapted to geophysical prospecting by Baron Roland von Eötvös, Professor of Physics at the University of Budapest. The Eötvös balances, first designed in 1888, were able to detect the small local variations often due to buried mineral deposits. Other geophysicists improved the apparatus over many years. It was made smaller and sturdier as the beam-length and weights were reduced. Photographic registration speeded up each operation and different layouts of beam and weights were designed for particular surveys.

Other arrangements using torsion or springs to counterbalance a small weight have led to the modern portable apparatus of today.

Threlfall Gravity Balance, 1900
Overall length: 65 cms

Designed by R Threlfall and J C Pollock as an alternative to pendulum methods. The responsive element is a horizontal quartz thread with a gilded brass cross-wire fastened slightly off-centre. With the element adjusted to balance the earth's gravity at a place where the absolute value is known, the instrument will respond to variation elsewhere by a slight twist of the wire and thread. The element, together with a platinum resistance thermometer, are encased under partial vacuum within insulated metal cylinders. The torsion angle is read with an attached microscope and vernier.

A number of observations were made in Australia with this balance.

Inv. no. 1932-493
Neg. nos. 611/61, 612/61, 613/61, 1402/76
Source: Lent by Sir Richard Threlfall

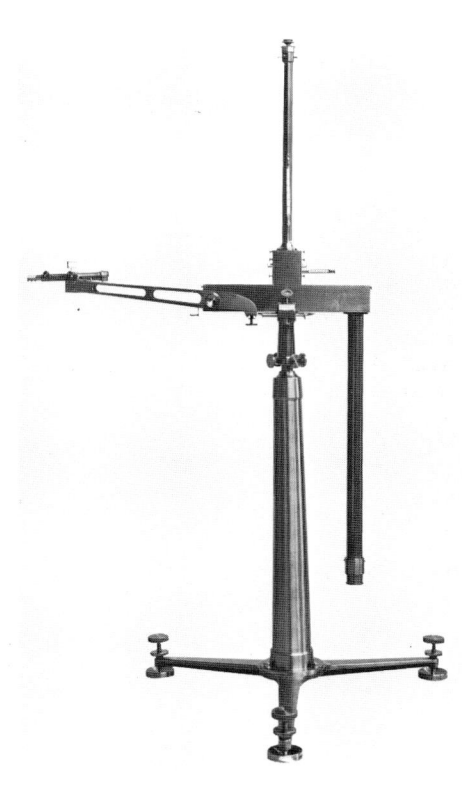

Eötvös Torsion Balance, 1920
Overall height: 192 cm
Made by Süss Nandor, Budapest
See also: 1928-1331, sectioned model, scale 1:2 of Eötvös Torsion Balance, page 40.

The aluminium balance beam is suspended on a platinum torsion wire and carries at either end platinum weights hanging at different levels. The beam assembly is housed in a double-walled brass case to shield it from any effects of temperature or electrical interference. This entire assembly can rotate horizontally. Any variation in local gravity deflects the beam and twists the torsion wire which has a small mirror fastened to it. A telescope and scale project from the beam assembly. The observer sees the scale reflected in the mirror; the reading therefore corresponds to the beam's distortion by local gravity anomaly.

Inv. no. 1920-809
Neg. nos. 1391, 1392, 1393
Source: Purchased from the maker

Threlfall Gravity Balance, 1900

Eötvös Torsion Balance, 1920

Photovisual Eötvös Torsion Balance, 1925
Overall height: 190 cm
Made by L Oertling, London

Retains the standard dimensions of Eötvös. The beam assembly has a triple-walled insulated casing. When photographed directly, a clock controls the presentation and exposure of the photographic plates and the rotation of the balance through the sequence of azimuth positions. When observed visually, the balance is housed within a triple-walled tent with the observer reading through portholes.

Inv. no. 1926-38 Neg. nos. 2371, 2372
Source: Lent by the maker

Gravity Meter, c 1930
Overall height: 30 cm
Made by Cambridge Instrument Co. Ltd

Designed by H Shaw and E Lancaster-Jones. It has a circular beam with several masses arranged to eliminate the effects of curvature. One of these masses is raised above the beam close to the torsion head. As curvature values can be ignored, the free period of the beam is reduced and operations are speeded up. The general size of the apparatus is also reduced, making it more easy to handle on field surveys.

Inv. no. 1932-493 Neg. no. 4729, 4734
Source: Lent by the maker

Thyssen Gravity Meter, 1939
Overall height: 75 cm
Made by Seismos GmbH, Hannover

The instrument works on the principle of the spring balance. A quartz beam rests on a central knife edge, with a 20-gram platinum mass at one end counterbalanced by a spring at the other. When this assembly is freed by raising the beam's centre of gravity, the platinum mass responds to local gravity field and moves accordingly. This movement is read by a prism and microscope focussed on a vertical scale fixed to the mass. The spring is sensitive to temperature changes and is therefore contained, with a thermometer, in a lagged tube.

Inv. no. 1953-220
Source: Lent by Imperial College

Worden Gravity Meter, c 1970
Overall height: 27 cm
Made by Texas Instruments, USA.
Model 113 No 3

The basic mechanism is made entirely of fused quartz. It consists of a weight counterbalanced by a spring. Any variation in gravity acting on the weight deforms the spring and the amount of adjustment needed to restore it is read off from the adjustment dial and can be directly converted to milligals. The mechanism is supported in an evacuated chamber within a thermally-insulated case. The complete apparatus weighs only 6lbs and can be used on land or sea, being lowered to the sea bed in a watertight container and operated by remote control.

Inv. no. 1976-586
Source: Lent by Geophysical Service International

Miscellaneous

Eötvös torsion balance.
Scale model 1:2, sectioned.
Inv. no. 1928-1331
Source: Made in Science Museum Workshops

Photographs, Russian torsion balances, c 1924
a. System of the Physico-Mathematical Institute, Leningrad.
b. Short period; system of Paul Nikiforov.
c. Transporting the Nikiforov balance.
Inv. nos. 1928-973, 1928-974, 1928-975
Source: Given by Paul Nikiforov

Photographs, Askania torsion balances.
a. Z-beam type, 1926.
b. Inclined-beam type, 1933.
Inv. nos. 1936-43, 1936-44, 1928-975
Source: Given by Askania-Werke A.G.

2 Photographs, Süss torsion balances.
Inv. no. 1936-94
Source: Given by Dr G Steiner

Photographs, Canadian gravity surveys.
a. Askania Z-beam balance, c 1936
b. Gravity field operations.
Inv. nos. 1936-97, 1936-98
Source: Given by the Canadian Geological Survey

Photovisual Eötvös Torsion Balance, 1925

Gravity Meter, c 1930

Exploration magnetometers

A magnetic needle pivotted in either a horizontal or vertical plane will be susceptible to variation in the intensity of magnetic force at right angles to that plane. Since dip and variation are known for a given geographical position, the local magnetic anomalies can be detected and measured. Such anomalies may be due to buried ore bodies, to volcanic intrusions, or to certain sedimentary deposits. Even the smaller disturbances due to human interference can be traced, so that the method is often useful for archaeological surveys.

Thomson-Thalen Magnetometer, 1899
Overall height: 30 cm
Made by J Berg, Stockholm

Measures variations in vertical intensity. Two magnetic needles carried on a brass ring swing in a vertical plane about an axis which in use is set parallel to the magnetic meridian by means of the small upper compass. The dip of these needles is then counteracted by a central vertical magnet which can be raised or lowered by a screw thread. Lines engraved on the glass window show when the paired needles are horizontal, and the position of the compensating magnet can be read off against a scale.

Inv. no. 1928-134 Neg. no. 4835
Source: Given by the maker

Horizontal Field Balance, 1924
Overall height: 34 cm
Made by Askania-Werke AG, Berlin

Measures horizontal intensity by the extent that it tilts a vertical magnetic assembly swinging in the magnetic meridian. A pair of broad flat magnets hang on a vertical axis which carries an observing mirror and rests on a quartz knife-edge. This assembly, with copper damper and thermometer, is housed in a cork-lined aluminium alloy case. A collimator telescope with an intensity scale at its focus is read both directly and by reflection from the mirror system, but requires a temperature correction.

Inv. no. 1926-561 Neg. nos. 448/65, 1065/78
Source: Lent by the maker

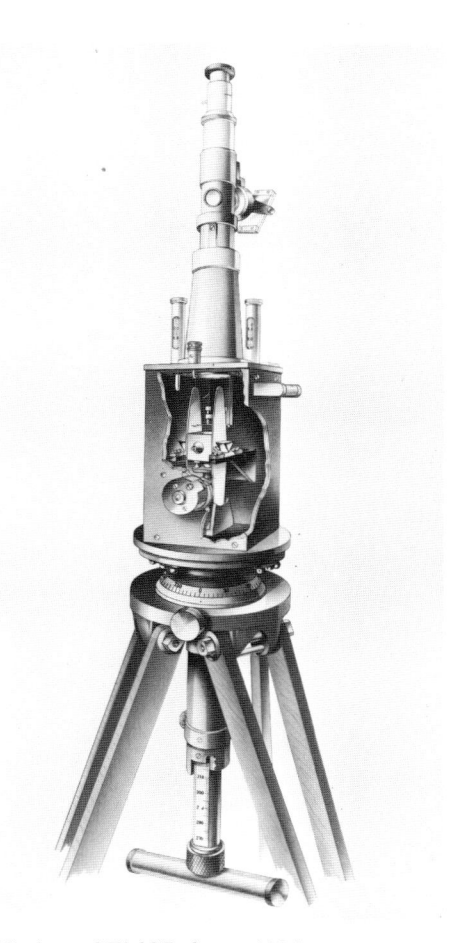

Horizontal Field Balance, 1924

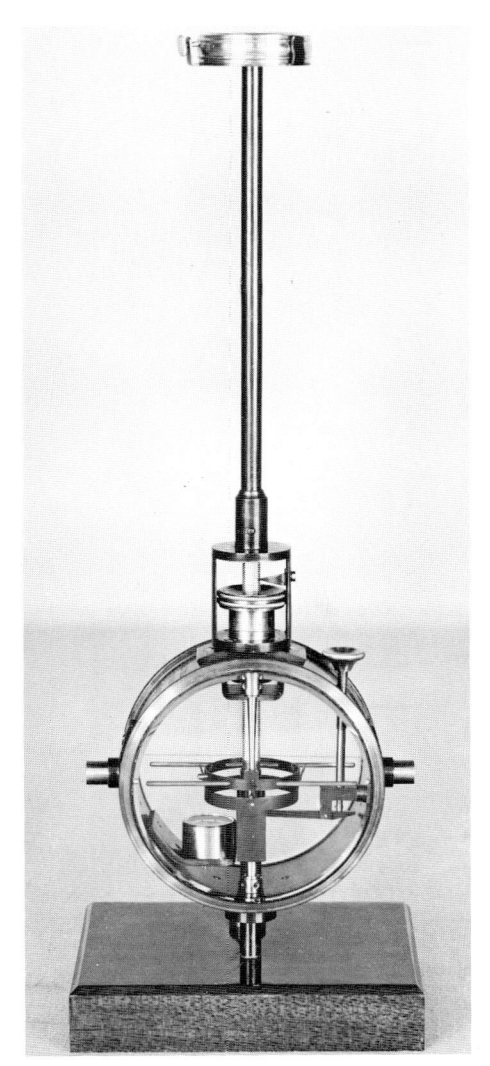

Thomson-Thalen Magnetometer, 1899

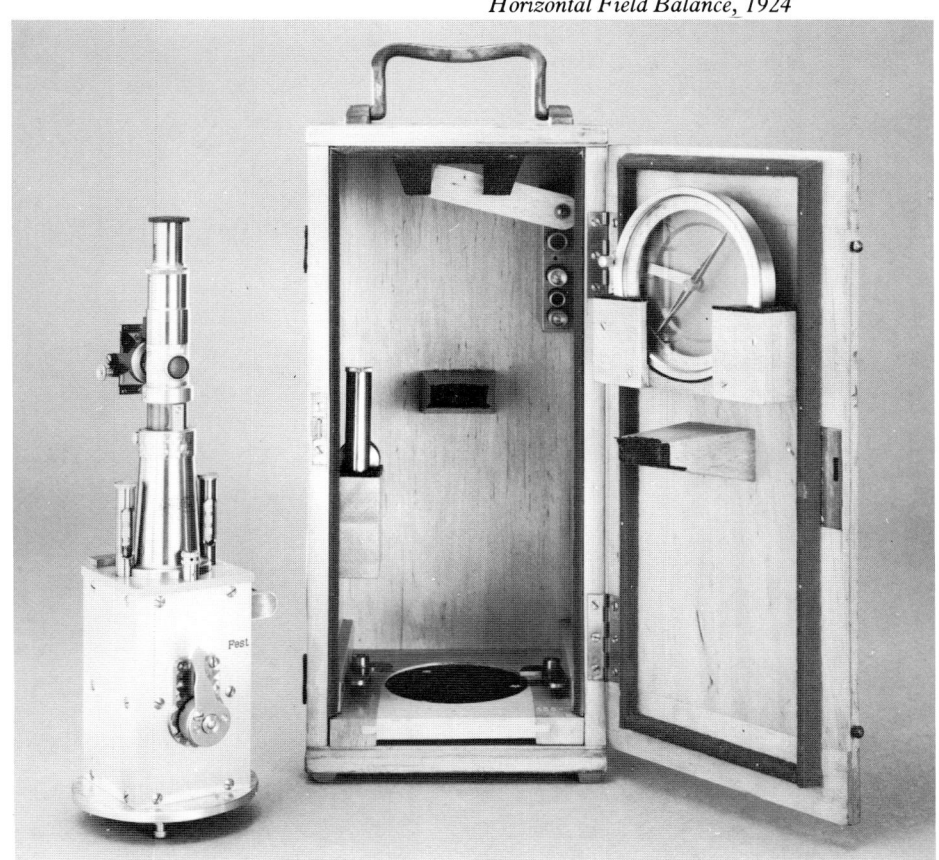

Thalen-Tiberg Magnetometer, 1928
Overall length: 56 cm
Made by J Berg, Stockholm

The apparatus combines Professor Thalen's magnetometer of 1882 (a compass with horizontal arm and deflector magnet), the dip compass of Tiberg, 1880, and an auxiliary deflector arm as devised by Dahlblom in 1898. Both dip and horizontal intensity can be rapidly measured in the field.

The compass box can be held in either plane. The magnet, rectangular in section, sharpened to knife edges at the poles, swings in cup bearings and has a sliding weight to counterbalance dip. The Dahlblom arm has a sliding carriage for the deflector magnet, and a graduated scale for measuring its distance from the compass.

Inv. no. 1928-135
Neg. nos. 4836, 4837, 4838, 4839
Source: Purchased from the maker

Vertical Force Variometer, c 1930
Overall height of variometer: 35 cm
Made by L Oertling Ltd, London

See 1935-540.

Inv. no. 1974-616
Source: Given by W H Fordham

Vertical Force Variometer, 1935
Overall height of variometer: 30 cm
Made by E R Watts & Son Ltd, No 15305

The magnet swings on a horizontal axis set to the magnetic meridian. It is balanced to lie horizontally in the earth's field in the survey area. Local changes of vertical field intensity tilt the system out of the horizontal in proportion to that intensity. The magnet assembly is enclosed within a cork-insulated case; an exterior mirror directs light onto the internal scale which is read through the telescope. A contained thermometer allows correction to be made for temperature change, while auxiliary magnets may be positioned below the casing to extend the range of measurement. Accuracy is ± 1 gamma. With reflecting head and recorder for photographic recording.

Inv. nos. 1935-540, 1935-541, 1935-542
Neg. nos. 4842, 4843, 4846, 4849
Source: Purchased from the maker

Vertical Force Variometer, 1935

Thalen-Tiberg Magnetometer, 1928

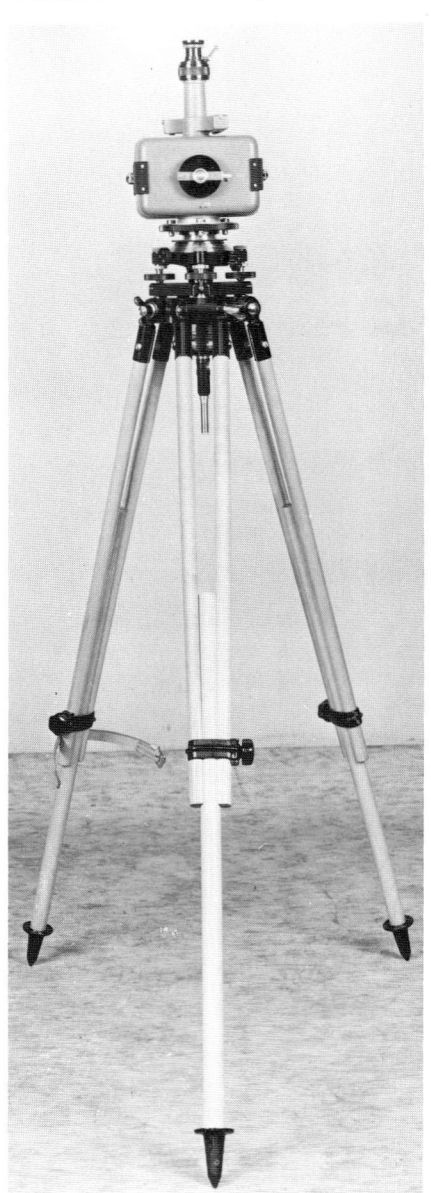

Airborne Fluxgate Magnetometer, 1951
Fluxgate head unit length: 18 cm
Made by Elliott Bros Ltd

Measures total magnetic force, subtracting the registered variations from an arbitrary datum. The sensing element, or fluxgate, is a core of mu-metal enclosed by a solenoid energised by an alternating current. The a.c. field saturates the core in opposite directions during alternate halves of the circle and as its energy drops between cycles the lines of force of the earth's magnetic field pass through the coil. In use, three fluxgates are mounted in gimbals and carried on a boom projecting behind the aircraft tail. The signal is rectified and amplified by the chassis units within the aircraft and the results are printed out on a paper chart. Accuracy is ± 2 gamma.

Inv. no. 1951-578
Source: Lent by the maker

Rubidium Magnetometer Sensing Element, c 1970
Overall length of displayed element: 19 cm
Made by Varian Associates, California

The element consists of a rubidium – vapour lamp, a filter to select one spectral line, a circular polariser, a rubidium – vapour cell and a photocell. The principles involved are optical pumping and the Zeeman effect. The cell is kept at maximum light absorption by radio frequency which is proportional to the energy differences of the Zeeman states and hence to the earth's magnetic field. Accuracy is ± 0.01 gamma.

Inv. no. 1978-424
Source: Lent by the maker

Proton Magnetometer, c 1970
Sensing element overall height: 14 cm
Made by Littlemore Scientific Engineering Co

Measures absolute value of total magnetic intensity. The sensing element is a bottle of water wound round with a coil. In the water protons (nuclei of hydrogen atoms) spin with their magnetic axes aligned to the earth's magnetic field. An intermittent strong magnetic field, at right angles to that of the earth, is applied to the water. As the protons reorient, a small voltage is induced in the coil, with a frequency proportional to the strength of the earth field. The accuracy is to within one gamma.

Inv. no. 1978-525
Source: Lent by the maker

Electrical prospecting methods

Practically all subsurface irregularities have electrical properties which differ from their surroundings. The proportion of groundwater, as well as the presence of certain metalliferous ores, increase conductivity, whereas loose dry sediments tend to decrease it. Equipotential lines of the electrical field within the earth are distorted near a body of material with a conductivity higher or lower than its surroundings. The methods used to search for these anomalies fall into two categories: *Spontaneous Polarization*, in which the natural field is measured, and *Resistivity*, which measures effects on an artificially applied field.

Electromagnetic (horizontal loop) Equipment, 1931

In the area to be prospected an alternating current, usually 500 cps, was maintained in the ground by an energised loop covering roughly ¼ sq mile. The current distribution, dependent on irregular subsurface conductivities, was investigated by moving a double-coil system across the ground. The coils were joined in opposition by an amplifier and headphones, or connected to a ratio arm bridge. Various ratios and aspects of the electromagnetic field could be plotted for the surveyed area.

Bieler – Watson double coil, 1931
Inv. no. 1931-800
Source: Made in the Science Museum Workshops

Spontaneous Polarization Equipment, 1931
Made by H Tinsley & Co, London

Small electrical currents, generated electrochemically, surround certain ore deposits. The phenomenon was first observed in Cornwall in 1830 by R W Fox and was soon developed to serve as a method of mineral prospecting.

Promising areas are tested by spacing non-polarizing electrodes in the ground along a traverse line and recording the potential gradients at regular distances from them. If an ordinary metal probe is used potentials are set up at the probe itself, which distort the result.

The equipment consists of a non-polarizing electrode and potentiometer. The electrode terminates in a porous pot which was filled with copper sulphate crystals and closed with a waxed cork. It was placed in a small hole in the ground and moistened if necessary to make good electrical contact.

The potentiometer, of a type designed by A B Broughton Edge, may also be used to measure resistivity and the delineation of equipotential lines.

Inv. nos. 1931-895, 1931-897
Source: Lent by the maker

Equipotential Equipment, c 1931
Hexagonal electrodes, 1925.
Potential ratiometer, c 1931.
Made by H Tinsley & Co London

A voltage applied to two electrodes inserted in the ground will cause a current to flow between them. In uniformly-conducting ground the lines of current flow follow a regular pattern similar to that around a bar magnet, and are at right angles to equipotential lines (lines of equal voltage) at the ground surface. Underground bodies of differing conductivity will distort the flow lines. A practical equipotential method was first devised in 1901 and used widely thereafter for mineral prospecting. Steel rapier electrodes feed alternating current into the ground and potential ratios are measured at uniform intervals between them. The character of the alternating field is represented by two series of lines known as equipotential and equiquadrature lines respectively.

A modification of the ratiometer originally designed by Broughton Edge in 1928 for use in Australia.

Inv. nos. 1931-898, 1931-896
Source: Lent by the maker

Resistivity Equipment

Current is fed into the ground through electrodes and distortion of the resulting potential field lines is measured, in terms of the gradient between the lines. Wenner described a field survey method in 1916. Various electrode configurations are used, to suit the purpose of the survey which may be mineral, engineering site, or archaeological prospecting.

Megger earth tester, c 1931, (sectioned model).
Contains a hand-driven generator, double commutator, and direct-reading dial which gives the ratio of two currents passing through two coils fixed together moving in a magnetic field.
Made by Evershed & Vignoles Ltd.
Inv. no. 1931-777
Source: Lent by H Tinsley & Co.

Tellohm resistivity meter
Nash & Thompson Ltd, Model GP, c 1960
Inv. no. 1980-678
Source: Given by Wimpey Laboratories Ltd.

Prototype Martin-Clark resistivity meter, 1956.

Designed for archaeological prospecting, one of the first meters to exploit the transistor for its compactness and low power requirements. With cranked electrodes, flex connections and headphones.

Inv. no. 1977-60
Source: Lent by the co-inventor, A J Clark

Martin-Clark resistivity meter, 1977.
Made by Location Instruments, Oxford.
With workboard and flex connections.
Inv. no. 1977-646
Source: Lent by the co-inventor, A J Clark.

Radiometric Equipment, c 1958

Natural radiation is emitted by uranium, thorium or radioactive potassium. The radioactive minerals may be concentrated in lodes or disseminated throughout large rock masses or sedimentary deposits.

Portable scintillation ratemeter, type 1413A. The detector is a thallium activated sodium iodide crystal. Gamma rays intercepted by the crystal produce minute scintillations which are multiplied within the collecting tube as an electron cascade and finally registered on a micro-ammeter dial or made audible through earphones.

Inv. no. 1958-229
Source: Lent by the Atomic Energy Research Establishment.

Miscellaneous

Model, 3′ × 3′, showing Archaeological Prospecting

Magnetic resistivity surveys being carried out at the site of Stenness.

Inv. no. 1978-9   Neg. no. 1489-78
Source: Purchased

Wilson's Magnetic Balance, 1918
Overall height: 53 cm.

Designed by Professor E Wilson for measuring magnetic susceptibilities of rock specimens and certain liquids. The balance depends for its action on the pull exerted by an electromagnet, balanced against the torsion in a phosphor-bronze strip. Disassembled.

Inv. no. 1931-232
Source: Lent by Kings College London.

Fifteen Rock Samples, Magnetically Investigated

Basalt, quartz porphyry and gabbro samples, tested for geological dating by Professor Koenigsberger.

Inv. no. 1938-222
Source: Given by Professor J G Koenigsberger, Freiburg.

Model, scale 1:24, showing underwater survey work
Length 160 cm, breadth, 70 cm, height 46 cm

Shows *Pisces* III and *Vol* LI submersible craft, and Pop-up bottom seismic recorder with buoyed mooring array. (Described in Seismic prospecting section, See 1977-42).

Inv. no. 1976-365
Source: Given by Vickers Ltd

Maker's Index

Adams, George   1910–127   27
Adie   1980–559   24
Askania-Werke AG   1926–561   41
Barrow, [H.]   1980–1883   31
Barrow, H & Co   1980–1879   31
Barrow, H & Co   1980–1880   31
Barrow, Henry & Co   1876–790   28
Bausch & Lomb   1975–38   23
Berg, J   1928–134   41
Berg, J   1928–135   42
Blunt, T   1917–109   28
Bosch, J & A   1932–440   6
Brassart   1884–63,64   2
Brunner Frères   1889–62   31
Brunner Frères   1889–63   28
Cambridge Inst Co Ltd   1932–493   40
Cambridge Sci.Inst.Co   1886–116   4
Cambridge Sci.Inst.Co   1888–173   3
Cambridge Sci.Inst.Co   1889–25   9
Cambridge Sci.Inst.Co   1891–99   20
Cambridge Sci.Inst.Co   1930–196   29
Charpentier, J   1884–58 to 62   34
Dollond   1876–805   30
Dover [A.]   1889–23   31
Dover [A.]   1930–195   31
Elliott Bros   1983–332   32
Elliott Bros   1926–284   11
Elliott Bros   1872–50   36
Elliott Bros   1951–578   43
English, John   1926–775   23
Evershed & Vignoles   1931–777   43
Fascianelli   1933–74   5
Foxboro-Yoxall   1975–382   23
Geophysical Service International   1978–423   38
Geophysical Service International   1978–422   38
Geophysical Systems Ltd   1984–674   38
George, W   1908–97   30
Geospace   1980-679   38
Griffin & Tatlock Ltd   1976–35   38
Grubb   1876–796   33
Kelvin & James White   1980–1875   12
Jones, Thomas   1914–586   17
Jones, Thomas   1914–587   18
Jones, Thomas   1902–142   18
Jones, Thomas   1902–143   21
Jones, Thomas   1915–144   32
Jones, Thomas   1980–1887   32
Jones, Thomas   1980–1890   32
Jones, W & S   1936–441   36
Légé & Co   1922–45   23
Légé, A   1881–13   24
Légé, A   1876–1129   24
Littlemore Scientific Engineering Co   1978–525   43
Location Instruments   1977–646   44
Masing, Hugo   1966–94   6
Munro, R W   1889–63   4
Munro, R W   1928–281   5
Munro, R W   1939–385   6
Munro, R W   1975–381   23
Nairne & Blunt   1900–129   29
Nairne & Blunt   1876–806   30
Nash & Thompson Ltd   1980–678   43
Oertling, L   1926–38   40
Oertling, L   1974–616   42
Pye, W G & Co Ltd   1955–1   38
Richard Frères   1935–203   15
Richard, J   1927–430   24
Robinson [T.C.]   1914–146   28
Robinson [T.C.]   1980–1885   28
Robinson [T.C.]   1876–804   30
Robinson [T.C.]   1980–1882   30
Robinson [T.C.]   1900–79   30
Robinson [T.C.]   1876–789   30
Robinson [T.C.]   1980–1881   30
Robinson & Barrow   1915–145   30
Schulze, G   1976–649   34
Seismos GmbH   1931–766   38
Seismos GmbH   1953–220   40
Spindler & Hoyer   1928–280   5
Stuckrath   1900–115,116   19
Süss Nandor   1920–809   39
Texas Instruments   1976–586   40
Tinsley, H & Co   1931–895   43
   1931–897   43
Tinsley, H & Co   1931–896   43
   1931–898   43
Union Radio Co Ltd   1981–825   36
Varian Associates   1978–424   43
Watts, E R & Son Ltd   1935–540 to 542   42
White, James   1885–115   3
White, James   1911–210   12
White, James   1927–206   11
White, James   1876–787   12
White, James   1881–12   24
White, James   1946–216   36